Love Me
With
Stubborn Love

Other books by Anne Ortlund

The Gentle Ways of the Beautiful Woman
Disciplines of the Beautiful Woman
Children Are Wet Cement

The Why's and
How's of Small Groups

Anne
Ortlund

Love Me
With
Stubborn Love

toExcel
San Jose New York Lincoln Shanghai

Love Me With Stubborn Love

Published by toExcel
an imprint of iUniverse.com, Inc.

For information address:
iUniverse.com, Inc.
620 North 48th Street
Suite 201
Lincoln, NE 68504-3467
www.iuniverse.com

ISBN: 0-595-00188-2

Printed in the United States of America

To the memory of my parents,
Brigadier General and Mrs. Joseph B. Sweet,
and my brother, Captain Robert E. Sweet;
and in appreciation to my sisters,
Mary Alice Keller and Margaret Wright.
Thank you, Lord, for the shapings of early years,
. . . for the joy of present fellowship.

Contents

Prologue

In front of me are letters: formal ones, business ones, letters written on notebook pages, letters written on table napkins and the backs of pictures, pink ones, blue ones, some penciled on scruffy paper, some on stationery crinkled with dried tears . . .

They're all great, every one. They're from the readers of my last book,[1] and over the last year and a half they've grown to be a chorus of voices with a strongly recurring theme:

"Thanks for what you had to say, Anne, but explain more about discipling. How do you go about it?"

"How do you start, to get a local bunch of Christians together?"

"Do you have any instruction sheets you give out to train your small accountability groups?"

"How do you help believers love each other? Is it possible, and are you supposed to?"

"Do you have a special outline you use in your discipling groups?"

"A group of us are willing to meet, but what do we do when we're together?"

The men write, too—honest!

"I bought your book for my wife, . . . but now I've got more disciples ready to go than she does. . . ."

"The notebook was the easy part, but your real challenge to me was to make more of a spiritual impact on other lives. Any more specific suggestions?"

Sometimes the cries are as urgent as this:

"Help, help! I have just finished your book, . . . and there are some young women who want and need discipling, but I don't know how to do it. . . . It sounds so exciting, I can hardly wait to get started, and the need is so great. . . ."

The hunger for meaningful Christian togetherness has grown enormous in today's world. And I think the hunger is intensified by the fact of our actual shyness, our inhibitions, our clumsiness in handling each other.

Think about your average married partners. In their minds are wild, wonderful dreams of how they'd like to treat each other, sizzling straight off the pages of novels! But in reality? They'd be terrified of anything a cut above tepid and predictable.

Don't you think most of us Christians are the same? We love to talk and dream "relationships," but in actuality our own often seem to be self-serving, phoney, disappointing, or at least just unappealing.

We need to look hard at the Bible's kind of love.

It's realistic.

It's tender.

It's aggressive.

It's tenacious.

It's jealous.

It's forever.

It's emotional.

It's total.

It's unspeakably sweet.

It's tough!

God loves us with tough love . . . and that's the way we need to learn to love each other.

God help us!—sometimes it's hot in there among Christians. There's flak and friction close in there together, because when it's biblical, it's tough. But there's also glory in there together, because when it's biblical, it's real love.

I pray that this book will be a textbook, a study guide, if God wills, to put the world-wide family of God together in tough love.

It's not that I know so much—but the last decade should have taught me something! My husband, Ray, and I have had ten years in the laboratory of hundreds of small groups in the Lake Avenue Congregational Church in Pasadena, California, where he's been pastor for twenty years. What we've learned by trial and error, the "how-to's" of small groups, I'll pass on to you in the last half of this book.

But the first half?

As I've watched God's precious family wrestle with all the relationship issues, both at home and around the world, "the burden of the Lord" is upon me. The contents of a book is in my heart, and woe is me if I don't get it on paper!

Part of what I write will appear controversial because it's "tough." I'm praying you won't take it out of context, without the "love"! I tell the Lord I have no desire to seem more tough than loving. The Holy Spirit is accurate but gentle. Jesus walked on two feet: grace and truth. I struggle to give this presentation God's balance.

Have you any idea of the birth pangs of a book? Help, somebody—pass me another pain pill!

1.

Love Is in the Air

My head is crammed with "together" memories:

The electric morning when 600 of us at the Lake Avenue Congregational Church vowed to reshape our lives to three priorities: to put God first in our lives, individually and as a church; to put each other in God's family second in priority; and to put our needy world third.[1] These three priorities caused a revolution for many of us then, and for hundreds more by now. . . .

Eight of us around our dining table looking into each others' eyes and singing, "May the Lord, mighty Lord, bless and keep you forever," to the tune of "Edelweiss." . . .

Joanne and I on her living room couch, after a misunderstanding, holding hands and crying as we prayed and got it all put back together again. . . .

A hundred or so missionaries in a jungle base in Ecuador as they unrolled around the whole room a giant swath of white butcher paper—paper covered with hundreds of greetings to them from our own church members in far-away California. . . .

A Christian friend close and precious to me pointing out a glaring fault of mine because it hurt both of us, and the "agony and the ecstasy" we both felt. . . .

Two of us kneeling in our living room, as six others laid hands on us before we went away to speak together for the Lord to another group for the weekend. . . .

Ray and I with our son Nels in 1972 kneeling before a thousand or so of our church people, as we were commissioned to represent them for three months in Afghanistan. . . .

And the love gifts that ebb and flow between us all as a result:

Ray's watch from financially pressed missionaries in Vietnam during the war. . . .

Clothes for Nels beautifully sewn by a woman who loves him for Jesus' sake. . . .

A dark suit we bought for a Christian brother. . . .

Hundreds of dollars some young couples insisted we take for unexpected air tickets to my parents' funerals. . . .

A check we mailed to a teenager who'd smashed her car. . . .

And—imagine—a check from a Christian friend who bought out our whole yard sale when she heard we were trying to get a piano. . . .

Have you got a headful of "together" memories? Christians all around you are waiting for your input, lonely for your love, hungry for what you know about Christ that they don't yet know.

I want a lot more "togetherness," too! The point is to expose myself to the right people at the right places and at the right times. That's what this book is all about: how to find those people, and how to put your life together with them when you do.

I'm looking at a piece of paper here in front of me: a list of thirteen ways the New Testament tells us to communicate with each other as Christian believers. When you eliminate the repetitions, did you know they boil down to only thirteen? Here they are:

1. Suffering together: 1 Corinthians 12:26.
2. Rejoicing together: Romans 12:15.
3. Carrying each others' burdens: Galatians 6:2.
4. Restoring each other: Galatians 6:1.
5. Praying for one another: Romans 15:30.
6. Teaching and admonishing each other: Colossians 3:16.
7. Refreshing one another: Romans 15:32.
8. Encouraging each other: Romans 1:12.
9. Forgiving one another: Ephesians 4:32.
10. Confessing to one another: James 5:16.
11. Being truthful with one another: Ephesians 4:25.
12. Spurring one another toward good deeds: Hebrews 10:24.
13. Giving to one another: Philippians 4:14, 15.

The question written at the bottom of the page says this: "Have I placed myself so deeply within a living, functioning local body that I myself am functioning in all these ways, and so living as a well-rounded, healthy, contributing member of the Body of Christ?"

My eye goes back to "suffering together." There was a time when Bill, a pastor we know, had his heart set on his congregation's adopting a plan for reorganization. The plan was voted down. Maybe it wasn't a good plan, but Bill was very tired, and it would have made his work load more bearable. Bill's wife, Julie, says she slipped out a side door, leaned against the church wall and sobbed out loud. But her misery wasn't alleviated, because she needed the "fellowship of suffering." She made her way to Bill's study, and there were Bill and two of the committee members who'd worked so hard on that plan. To hear them tell it now, the four of them cried so hard together, their noses ran together!

Or "rejoicing together." I remember 1 Corinthians 12:26, "If one part [of the Body] is honored, every part rejoices with it," and I think of tall, black-haired George. Not only did he coach his high school basketball team to championship, but he and Danita led every member of the team to accept Christ; that following Sunday night at church, how the Christians crowded around him, laughing and shouting, hugging and kissing him! His honor was their honor, and George loved sharing it with them. That was a yahoo-time for everybody.

Or "restoring one another." I think of Sharon's pleading with a Christian sister to break her engagement to an unbeliever. Sharon was demonstrating "tough love"—caring enough to act.

Or "giving to one another." When I slip into a certain peach flannel robe, I feel absolutely wrapped up in love. It was worn by, and given to me by, a friend in Christ.

You have to "place yourself deeply" within a living, functioning local body to begin to give and take at deep levels.

Hear that phrase well! You must "place yourself deeply." If you run off weekends to recreate, or stay home some Sundays and catch church by television, or even dip here and there into other churches as a visitor and think you've done it, you pay a terrible price. Your fellow believers move in to each other and close the gap, and they learn to get along without you. There is no substitute for constant, faithful exposure to your own local family of God. The sweetest surprises in fellowship come to Mr. and Mrs. Faithful, who show up whenever the others show up.

That's your part—but it's a two-way thing. Your church has to be "living and functioning." How can you tell if you're in the right church? It need not be large, and it will not be perfect! But it must be alive and functioning. As Sam Shoemaker once said, "You can't put a live chick under a dead hen!"

Ray and I once went way back into a remote cranny of the

Himalayan mountains to help three women there become a "living, functioning" part of the Body of Christ. The three were the only Christians there, ministering medically to the mountain peasants. We talked to them about vital worship together, about stimulating each other to good works, about making God and each other priorities above their work. One, an East German, just sat silently and wept, God bless her. But for those women to continue in spiritual and physical health in that very hard place, it was imperative for their "church" of two or, hopefully, three to be "living and functioning."

A local church, no matter how small, to be the right place for you, must be not only a place where you can minister, but where you can be ministered to. It must work both ways! Don't wear yourself out in service trying to hang on because they "need" you (need you for what?), if there's not enough life in the Spirit there for them to pour back into you. Jesus says, "Where two or three are gathered *in my name*"—not just gathered—that he will be in the midst, and his presence will be felt and known. (Of course, I'm speaking to those in areas of the world where Christians have the luxury of choosing between several churches!)

On the other hand, don't be too proud or too shy or too preoccupied to receive the life when it's there! Or perhaps it's truly there, but undisclosed. Many church people are like that alabaster vase of perfume in Mark 14:3. They have the true Gospel of Christ in their hearts; they're full of potential; but they're tight and closed up, not knowing how to love each other.

We need to learn to love! In my own experience, I grew up in a Christian home and was a pastor's wife for years before the biblical principles of how to love began to be translated in my mind into practical outworking. And these principles have caused me to open up to a new life I'd never known before.

Faces come to my mind: Martha, Sally and Nancy, Betsy, Jim, Elaine, Lee, Linda, Dick, Lu—and so many more whom I never could have known well if I hadn't had some tools at hand to make it happen.

Thank you, Lord! You have made me rich in friends. They're friends who know me well—my sins and failures, too— and they still love me. Please give these readers the tools to forge this kind of Christian friendships, which will make them courageous to live for you as they never could have otherwise done. Make this book the doorway to lives rich in eternal relationships. . . .

When I wrote those few names just now, I cringed because I was missing so many! But then I remembered Romans 16 and took courage. Paul, the writer, was a traveler and could easily have been a loner. But whether it was easy or not, he saw to it that he made his way deeply into the lives of many other believers. In his letter to the Romans he greets specific people by name, at the risk of omitting many others. He names twenty-seven men and eight women.

He mentions Phoebe, a business woman traveling to Rome who carried his letter for him. (Donald Barnhouse wrote, "The Reformation was in that luggage!")

He mentions Aquila and Priscilla, a married couple in business together, who often traveled with Paul. How he loved those two!

He mentions Erastus, city treasurer of Corinth. In 1929 a pavement was uncovered which is inscribed to say that Erastus "laid this pavement at his own expense." Erastus was a Christian "big shot."

He mentions Tertius, his scribe. If Paul's eyes were bad, what must Tertius's have been, after all that workout? But Tertius was willing simply to serve Paul by writing his letters.

In other words, Paul mentions big people, little people, women, men, all kinds—probably all shapes and sizes. He got deeply into their lives. He knew them and loved them well.

"I love the church!" Ray exclaimed to me recently. I know it's true. He loves the grandparents, the children, the middle-agers, the young people; he loves the mystics, the pragmatists, the theologians, the simplists, the immature and the deep, the visionaries and the plodders, the faithful committee workers who make it happen and the laggards who have to be cajoled. Ray loves the church! I can't pray he'll back off; I can only pray he'll have the body and heart to love it for a long, long time.

And as his wife, I see what the church has done for Ray—deep things I never could have done.

I told this to a young wife recently, who didn't want her husband to serve on one of our church committees. "Let your husband go," I said. "Don't try to overpossess him. If you don't sense that he's deliberately escaping from his family, which is another matter—then (I know this sounds heretical) let him plunge into all the church life he wants to. His heart may need it. Encourage lots of exposure to godly people. He'll be a far better husband and father as a result!"

(Insert: I could never have said this if our church were not a "living and functioning" organism. That's why finding the right church is crucial.)

I told her how the multifaceted, richly diverse Body of Christ has stretched and challenged Ray in a thousand ways I couldn't—ever—as one human being. Those men collectively know things I'll never know; and they communicate their godliness to Ray as only godly men can communicate to each other. And the women, too: how he needs the richness of many Christian sisters in his life! This has nothing to do with his marriage relationship; after all those committees, I'm the one he comes home to! (Yea!) But there have been times when he's come home and, for all the fatigue, there's a look of splendor shining in his eyes. (Once he came home and said to me, "Anne, I was discouraged. And they laid their hands on me and recommissioned me to my life's work. It was a holy, glorious time!")

And because of all that wonderful input of his brothers and sisters in Christ—when he does come home, in less time, he's a far more effective husband and father. Oh, yes! The children and I wouldn't trade.

The miracle of the church! Who can explain it? We need all the relationships God will give us. Each believer represents a different facet of Jesus Christ; and as we are baptized into a life of fellowship in the Spirit, we are plunged into Christ himself. Doctrinally, we are baptized into Christ at the moment of our conversion. Experientially, you might say that we are "baptized" into Christ as we are daily immersed in our fellow believers.

"Yuck!" somebody reacts. "You mean John and Susie and Pete and Sally, all my dumb ol' buddies—uh, of whom I am their dumb ol' buddy?"

Right, right! God *said* it would be a miracle!

"From him the whole body," says Ephesians 4: 16, "joined and held together by every supporting ligament, grows and builds itself up in love, as each part does its work."

Friend, we need to lay down our arms. We need to take a vow as seriously as our marriage vow that we will love the church, "for better and for worse, in sickness and in health, until death do us part."

But that verse in Ephesians won't happen unless each part does its work. We need the tools by which we forge meaningful relationships in the Body of Christ. This book, God helping me, is to share with you some of those tools.

2.

Are These the "Last Days"?

Bill teaches our Sunday school class. Every Sunday he tells us a new joke. We laugh even before he gets to the punch line just because we love Bill so much.

Bill leans over the podium grinning. "The father says, 'Do you think buying Junior a bicycle will improve his behavior?' The mother says, 'No, I don't think it will, but it will spread it out over a larger area.'"

Another Sunday arrives. "Have you heard about the new product that just came out?" says Bill. "It's a toothpaste that has shoe polish mixed with it for people who keep putting their foot in their mouth."

I wouldn't say anybody comes to Mariners' Class just to catch Bill's gentle humor, but *something* brings us. Something brings 175 of us. Last fall attendance was pushing 200, so we spawned a baby class. Come to think of it, the new class doesn't even *hear* Bill's jokes, and they've grown to over 70!

What is it that's so exciting these days about "Body life"? Why are Christians so hungry to relate to each other that theologians lean back in their swivel chairs and talk about "relational theology"? How come it turns *me* on? Believers expressing their love of God together even beats a Dodgers game.

And what's all this with small groups, that has made the movement one of the powerful social phenomena of our times?

I suspect maybe it's the patter of raindrops beginning to fall.

Back in the early days, the "promised land" that God gave to the Israelites was like Kansas. Nowadays it's like Arizona, but God promises it will be a Kansas again! What do I mean? Well, there used to be two rainy seasons a year in Israel, the early rains and the latter rains. The early rains started around November with some preliminary showers; then intermittent falls, lasting two or three days each, continued through December, and more or less through the rest of the winter. That was the plowing and planting season mentioned in Proverbs 20: 4. Then with the approach of harvest, really heavy rains returned, and these were the "latter rains" of ingathering.

Two rainy seasons a year were God's reward for good behavior (Deut. 11:13–14), and made the place like Kansas. Bethlehem, you remember, means "house of bread," and was part of the wheat and barley fields harvested so richly by Boaz and Ruth and others.

But God kept warning the Israelites that if they continued in deliberate sin, he would withdraw the spring rains (Jer. 3:3; 5:24–25). They did, and he did—and the land gradually became a rocky, dry Arizona. And so it is today, although the recently returned Jews have brought with them modern irrigation techniques.

But the big difference will come when God really makes the newly ingathered Jews the center of his world of righteousness and justice (Ezek. 34:11–13), and returns to the land of Israel its spring rains (Ezek. 34:26). Then the earth will really "yield its crops" (v. 27), as he expected it to do from the beginning, and Israel will again be "good pasture" for God's Jewish flock (v. 14).

Mr. Aaron is our local children's barber, and he cut our son Nels's hair the first twelve years of his life. Mr. Aaron has beautiful blue eyes with pain in them. He makes funny noises to entertain the kids, and expertly snips their hair even if they turn unexpectedly. You hear a bird chirp—up comes an arm with scars on it from being a Jew in Poland—and a little cherub, innocent of all the world's problems, gets a beautiful haircut.

I love Mr. Aaron. We have talked deeply sometimes about Jesus and about being Jewish.

"I honor you, Mr. Aaron," I tell him. "God chose you to be his special people, and he never breaks his promises. One day there'll be a great world revival and turning to God. You people will be the world's 'big shots,' with everyone else hanging on you to learn about your God. You've got your finest days ahead of you!"

Mr. Aaron's blue eyes watch me wistfully as he listens, and he reads the Old Testament between customers.

The prophet Joel comforted Israel with the same predictions:

> "Be glad, O people of Zion,
> rejoice in the Lord your God;
> for he has given you
> a teacher for righteousness.
> He sends you abundant showers
> both autumn and spring rains as
> before. . . .
> And afterward,
> I will pour out my Spirit on all people.
> Your sons and your daughters will prophesy,
> your old men will dream dreams,

> your young men will see visions.
> Even on my servants, both men and women,
>   I will pour my Spirit in those days.
> I will show wonders in the heavens and on the earth,
>   blood and fire and billows of smoke.
> The sun will be turned to darkness
>   and the moon to blood
>   before the coming of the great and dreadful day of
>   the Lord.
> And everyone who calls
>   on the name of the Lord will be saved" (Joel 2:23,
>   28–32).

Ten days after Jesus' ascent back into heaven, on the day of Pentecost, the early rains of Holy Spirit revival descended. They were wonderful; three thousand people accepted Christ in one day, and in those powerful moments the church was born.

And Peter deliberately linked what was happening with Joel's prophecy. He quoted in Acts 2:16–21 the very passage from Joel I've just quoted to you. But in that amazing prophecy, God the Spirit had done what he so often does: he blended two events into one, so you can't do a good job of separating them except by hindsight.

Joel put together the early rains and the latter rains, and Peter quoted the whole prediction, when, actually, he could have stopped with Joel 2:29. On the day of Pentecost there was certainly prophesying, but there were no wonders in the skies; the sun didn't turn to darkness or the moon to blood. Those things haven't happened yet.

The past almost two thousand years have been like Israel's winter time following the early rains. There have been occasional "falls" of the Holy Spirit's blessing here and there. But the Bible predicts a latter rain of revival which will really be some "gusher," compared to the revival connected with Jesus' first coming. That one affected only one city, Jerusalem; this will affect the whole world (Matt. 24:14). That affected a few thousand people; this will affect unnumbered multitudes (Isa. 45:22–23). That was an authentic rain, for sure, but small compared with the spring rain that will come.

D. M. Patton writes,

> Vastly more was wrapped up in the descent of the Holy Spirit than the church has yet experienced, or than the world has yet seen; and the Spirit himself thus reveals that while the Christian centuries are "the last days," and Pentecost began the wonder, we today, standing in the last of the last, are on the edge of a second and more tremendous upheaval of the Holy Spirit.[1]

Why do I say that maybe the patter of raindrops is now beginning to fall?

Well, rainy seasons may be light or heavy, but they certainly do have similarities. And I submit that there has never been such renewed interest in the lifestyle of the early church, or such zeal in patterning after it, as there is today. We're tired of the crusting over of traditions and pomp and rote. We're eager to recapture the simplicity and reality of the first!

Study carefully chapters 2 through 7 of Acts. Beginning at chapter 8 persecution scattered the Christians, and they could never again live and worship under ideal circumstances. But particularly in Acts 2–4 we have a description of the believers, in the first fullness of the Holy Spirit, living exactly the way he led them to, without any outside interference.

That was pure, "in-the-Spirit" living! They weren't perfect. They were people just like us. But they were blessed to live during the drenching of the early rains of the Spirit.

Does your heart leap up to hear about those early Christians? Do you long to identify with them, and be part of a "people-movement" which rediscovers authentic Christian lifestyles?

Do you feel yourself getting wet? Or wanting to get wet?

3.

Our Models for Living

Acts 2:42–47 is the kind of lifestyle God could help many of his people to recapture today, probably you. It doesn't call for communes, or any special circumstances. Listen to how they lived:

> They devoted themselves to the apostles' teaching and to the fellowship, to the breaking of bread and to prayer. Everyone was filled with awe, and many wonders and miraculous signs were done by the apostles. All the believers were together and had everything in common. Selling their possessions and goods, they gave to anyone as he had need. Every day they continued to meet together in the temple courts. They broke bread in their homes and ate together with glad and sincere hearts, praising God and enjoying the favor of all the people. And the Lord added to their number daily those who were being saved.

We can't work up the miracles, or even the awe! But let's look at this very human and very real scene. What a "togetherness" passage! Talk about Body life! We're struck right away with the fact that they spent a lot of time together.

Three thousand were new baby Christians. One hundred and twenty were former believers. "They," verse 42, means all of them, former and new, living out the new lifestyle together.

"They devoted themselves." Catch the intensity! And remember, these were real people like us. They still had jobs to hold down; they still had to clean their houses and wipe the babies' noses and do everything that normal people have to do. But they *wanted* to be together, so they *got* together. That's living by priorities.

Let me quickly say that when they were in this first "rain" of the Holy Spirit, the specialness of it was all God's doing. The work upon and in them was the Spirit's work and not their own. It would be simplistic and superficial to copy their external way of living and think we could pull the latter rains out of the skies and onto our heads!

God's work is God's work. We can't conjure it up ourselves; we only wait and long and pray for his timetable to bring Christ's return and its accompanying worldwide blessing.

But "signs of the times" indicate it may be near. And if God is preparing his people for the "latter rains," let's study the characteristics of the "former rains" and be open, expectant, and obedient to all his Spirit's promptings!

What kind of life did those first Christians live? When they were together, they devoted themselves to four things. John Calvin wrote in his *Institutes:* "We must endeavor to keep and preserve this order, if we will be judged faithful to the church before God and the angels."

First, they gave themselves to "the apostles' teaching." That was everything the apostles had seen Jesus do and heard him say. Eventually they got it all written down; now we call it the New Testament. Our equivalent today of the "apostles' teaching" would be Bible study.

Second, they devoted themselves to the fellowship. That was

simply being together for the joy of being together. Why draw your stimuli for life, they must have been thinking, from non-Christians who have nothing to contribute, when you could be absorbing more and more of the life of Christ from within your Christian friends? This was no deliberate cut-off from worldlings to be exclusive. Their fellowship was the strong base from which they reached out to others. But there was far more power for evangelism in this close-knit community than we find today—we, whose spirits are diluted by so much exposure to the world—even though we may say it's to win them for Christ!

Third, they devoted themselves to breaking bread together. I'm sure this meant Communion, but I think it meant other meals, too. How did it happen? Well, I'll use my imagination. Here was Thomas with a roomful of new believers in a home together. They were singing, praying, laughing together, sharing their trials, and listening to Thomas teach. Finally one of them slaps his forehead.

"I don't believe it!" he says. "The sun's gone down. I hadn't even noticed. The children must be starving."

Everybody looks shocked and frustrated. The lady of the house says, "Oh, Thomas, just keep talking, and I'll break out something for us, somehow."

Another woman speaks up, "I couldn't resist hoping we'd go overtime, and I packed some bread and yogurt for us, just in case. . . ."

My bet is that the meals just *happened* that way at first, and they added so much to the fun and close feelings, besides extending the time, that they began to be planned for!

Number four ingredient in their new life together: "the prayers." That's right, the Greek has the article *the* in front of it, and it's the same word as in Acts 3:1: "One day Peter and John were going up to the temple at the time of the prayers." In other words, "the prayers" were the stated times for worship in the temple, and all the believers went together.

Probably the temple leaders didn't even know Jesus as their Messiah; the Christians went because their Savior had regularly gone (Luke 4:16), and because they saw that the habit of faithful "churchgoing" was a righteous habit, and by it they spurred each other toward good deeds (Heb. 10:24–25). There were the spontaneous meetings around the Lord in homes, which were wonderful. But there were also the stated, regular public gatherings—whether you felt like it or not—when you fit into the schedule of all, for the common good, instead of your own schedule. And those experiences had their own special glory, and still do, whether felt or not.

No doubt a lot of former activities had to go, for the early Christians. They "eliminated" and they "concentrated"; they "continually devoted themselves" to these four things.

Friends, let's check our lifestyles. Have we eliminated a lot of clutter from our lives so that we, and the ones around us who want to go hard after God, can give ourselves to Bible study, to fellowship, to eating together, and to the regular services of the church?

That's the way they lived in the early rain of revival.

And there's more. Their money and their possessions were immediately affected, the sure proof that their hearts were changed. Don't think that these verses in Acts 2 indicate some kind of communism! Though the system employed here worked so well that later, briefly, the "common kitty" idea went further, here the Greek verb tells us that it wasn't some once-for-all act when everybody gave up his private possessions. No, they "began selling . . . and sharing . . . as anyone might have need" (Acts 2:45, NASB).

Here was Bartholomew, who got laid off his job. "H'mm," thought Tertius. "Just when he's growing so well in Christ, the devil would love to distract him and discourage him. Now I know, Father, why you gave me that tract of land I've been holding on to. Its price can tide over Bartholomew until he gets the right new job and everything can go along smoothly for him. What a thrill that I can help! Praise the Lord!"

Because they gave, they loved. And because they gave, they *were* loved. Giving to each other stimulated love in the Body.

The fullness of the Holy Spirit over a group makes claims of the group higher than the claims of the individual. This is always true in times of revival and times of God's special blessings upon a group. The Old Testament Israelites gave up their jewelry to build the tabernacle—and were thrilled to do it.

My friend, true Christianity is more than a verbal *explanation* of life. It is a *way* of life—a 24-hour-a-day, courageous, thrilling way.

Many people these days are accepting Christianity as an explanation of life, but they're not willing to accept it as a way of life. Lots of supposed "evangelical Christians" live lives no different from those of the world. We make too much of their intellectual assent—especially if they're rich or famous or charming! Christ calls us not only to accept an explanation, but to practice a way. That's tougher.

For one thing, it means meshing your life as closely as possible with other believers. No snobbery. No privileges. All together, sharing the same ideas (the apostles' doctrine), the same friends (fellowship), the same practices (breaking of bread), and the same religious habits (public prayers).

One of the young wives in our church was talking to me recently. She said, "Jerry and I have been praying over the passage that says if you have two coats, to give to him who has none. We discovered that we're now over the median income of our church members, so we're two-coat people, and that gives us the responsibility of caring for the others."

I said to her, "Do you remember, Linda, several years ago when Jerry was going through seminary, you were the no-coat ones; and how often believers would lovingly slip you money, or put a bag of groceries in the back door?"

She said, "Oh, *yes!* How could we forget? And now that it's the other way, we've upped our church giving, and we're also looking for the ones who need our help. They're all around us, and the Lord has already pointed out the first one."

She named a single mother raising teenagers, and she told gleefully about a sneaky plan to meet one of her needs anonymously. I couldn't help being tickled because she was so tickled!

Sharing in the family of God is a sure sign of authenticity. I love it when we get so comfortable with each other that we can think, "I do believe Sharon would look better in this sweater than I do; I think I'll offer it to her!" It's not a matter of charity as we now use the word—it's not who's richer and who's poorer; it's charity in its old usage—just pure love in the Body!

Judy and I were in a group together when her husband decided he didn't want her to wear pants suits or slacks any more. Judy said to me,

"Anne, I've got this really good pants suit, and we're just the same size. Do you want to try it on?"

I took it; I wore it; I loved it. But a few months later I began to notice Judy wearing pants again.

"How come?" I asked.

"Oh," she smiled, "he's over his 'pants' kick."

"Judy," I said "would you like your pants suit back again?"

Judy's eyes filled with tears. "Would you believe, I'm going up to San Francisco to visit my mother for a few days, and I didn't have a thing to wear, and I was wishing for it!"

Back went the pants suit, and Judy and I loved each other all the more for having shared it.

We've got to learn to "hang looser" about possessions in the family of God. There were lots of Old Testament laws even to legislate this kind of attitude!—

You weren't to charge interest on a loan to a fellow Israelite, only to a foreigner. (That meant one who didn't know God [Deut. 23:19–20]).

If you requested payment on a loan, you were to stand outside a fellow Israelite's house, not go in. Then you wouldn't seem too pushy (Deut. 24:10–11).

When you harvested your crops, you weren't to pick clean. You were to leave some fruit on the tree, or leave your fallen wheat on the ground, for the needy and the stranger (Lev. 19:9–10).

You were to pay salaries immediately, and pay any debts as soon as you had the money. You weren't to hold it when you had it (Deut. 24:15).

You could always eat freely from any neighbor's property what you could carry in your hand. You just couldn't bring your baskets! (Deut. 23:24).

And so on. So there was a strong sense of ownership, and pride of ownership and respect for ownership. But at the same time, the edges were to slop over and nobody was to get uptight about it. They were to learn to be generous and loose with each other—because God is that way with all of us!

We Christians have a lot to learn about this in very practical, nitty-gritty ways. We can't get close to everyone if our church is very large, but we ought to be close enough to some, that when payday is three days away and they've run short of cash, we know it and take care of it.

It's pretty important, then, that all the two-coat people not huddle in small groups together, and all the no-coat people in the other groups. We have to mix it up. George and Mary Helen are a comfortable, "establishment" couple in our church who deliberately put together a weekly group of believers who are diverse in every way: age, status, circumstances, and all. What a loving time they've had! That blesses me.

Well, Acts 2:46–47 are the wrap-up verses on early Christian lifestyle:

> Every day they continued to meet together in the temple courts. They broke bread in their homes and ate together with glad and sincere hearts, praising God and enjoying the favor of all the people. And the Lord added to their number daily those who were being saved.

We see two places where their lives were centered: in the temple courts (we would say church) and in homes. Who could fit in the church? Everybody. Who could fit in homes? Small groups. Their lifestyles included both kinds of togetherness.

How often did they get together? "Daily." (And we think we're so spiritual if we see each other twice a week!) Yes, they had been busy people before the Holy Spirit came into their lives. It was simply a matter of eliminating a lot of things that didn't matter much, now that eternity had come into view.

Verse 46 says that this lifestyle made for gladness, because it was selfless: "I will disciple you; I will love you; I will teach you; I will laugh with you and cry with you; I will eat with you; I will worship with you; and as you have need, I'll take care of you."

And verse 46 says that this lifestyle made for singleness of

heart, or sincerity of heart—both unity and open reality—
because it also said, "I expect you to love me, disciple me,
teach me, laugh and cry with me, eat with me, worship with
me, and care for me. We're all in this together. We're all
doing it."

No wonder verse 47 says that it made such a happy, vigorous
fellowship that from the three thousand in one day, the numbers just took off and kept soaring!

All that was a long time ago. And the former rains dimin-
ished and quit, and the world became spiritually dry. The
Dark Ages ensued. . . .

But half a millennium ago a monk named Martin Luther
rediscovered the meaning of faith. "The just shall live by
faith!" he read, and raindrops began to patter all around the
world.

Then a century or more ago, believers rediscovered the
meaning of hope. The Lord's return was the big news and the
big study, and from it missions sprang to life, and study edi-
tions of the Bible, and Bible schools and Bible conferences and
parachurch movements, and so on. More showers here and
there!

In this generation believers are rediscovering the meaning
of love. We are reaching for and finding each other. There are
new longings for unity: organizational unity by some, but
deeper than that. Denominational walls are breaking down.
"Share" is the word. "Small group" is where the action is.

Faith has been rediscovered. Hope has been rediscovered.
And now love is being rediscovered. But the greatest of these
is love!

The first Christians were bound together by the same doctrine (the apostles'), the same practices (fellowshiping and eating in each other's houses), the same worship habits (both at

church and in homes), and the same rights and responsibilities financially. This is a common lifestyle that's exciting; it takes courage; it's out on the cutting edge; it brings a lot of laughter to life; it's zingy; and it gives God pleasure!

Right now we're too rigid and organized when we try to copy it: "Be regular Sunday morning and evening." . . . "Get into a small group." . . . Still, that's better than doing nothing!

But study to recapture the spirit of this "together" lifestyle, and pray it in! Then make it "daily." Make it "accountable to." Make it "responsible for." Make it visible!

None of this "Well, I went to our cabin this Sunday, but I was with you in spirit." These people's *bodies* were continually with each other! When we were having meetings recently in Sacramento, Carol, a beautiful red-headed lady lawyer we love, came to the services after very full work days. Carol's smiling explanation was, "I believe if you get your 'bod' to the place of blessing, all the rest will follow!"

Are these the "last days"? Is Christ going to return soon? Are the latter rains of revival beginning to fall around the world? It would seem so, from happenings in Africa, South America, Korea, Indonesia, parts of the United States, and elsewhere.

But whether you're in the right geographical area or not, revival can come to you, personally. And to yours.

My friend Reudun has white-hot spiritual fire in her bones. I love her. She accepted Christ as a teenager in her native Norway, when revival was sweeping the land. She loves to describe how people talked about Jesus continually on the streets, in the markets, in homes; how they were continually fellowshiping with each other; how it was hard to break up the church meetings because nobody wanted to quit.

"Tell me, Reudun," I asked, "did everybody in Norway

become Christian in those days? Was it just sort of a blanket thing?"

"Oh, no!" she said. "Some people hardly knew it was happening. Most of the big state cathedrals went right on with their dry, empty services with a dozen little old ladies and hundreds of empty pews."

I thought of how a gusher of rain can make water pour down the side of a mountain; and if it should strike a big rock, it will just divide and go around it. And the rock will just sit there, as unmoved as though nothing were happening.

Dear friends, there's new life all around the world. There's excitement about Jesus; there's hunger to get back to the original Christian lifestyle; it's a new day!

Don't be one of those rocks. Don't let God's revival pass you by!

4.

Close to God's Heart

I was a speaker last year at a large denominational gathering, and before my time came, I sat listening to a fellow speaker. He preached from Psalm 127:1: "Unless the Lord builds the house, its builders labor in vain. Unless the Lord watches over the city, the watchmen stand guard in vain."

His exposition was that the verse said, "first the house, then the city," and he deduced from that, "first the family, then the church."

My heart was crying, "Heresy! Heresy!"

Soon it was my turn. I was speaking on the church, and there in my notes it came out—gulp! "Why is the church second in priority only to God himself?" It sounded like rebuttal, but, so help me, it was planned long before, and I didn't have any other notes along to use!

We had all turned to the first three chapters in Ephesians, and my notes listed four reasons why the Body of Christ is the second priority:

1. Because it preexisted in the heart of God before the world began (Eph. 1:4). "This is said of no other of God's institutions—the government, the family, or anything else," said my notes!

2. Because the church is Christ's gift to the Father (Eph. 1:11, 18). What does God get out of it, to have sent his Son to die on the cross? He gets us! And—hallelujah—he thinks that's wonderful!

3. Because the church is Christ's Body (Eph. 1:22–23). The church is his "fullness," his completion. In a truer way than Eve ever completed Adam, we complete Christ. He has put in his plan an absolute necessity for us. In a genuine sense, the church is not an organization but an organism.

4. Because the church is convincing evidence to the universe that God is merciful, good, and wise (Eph. 3:9–10); and this demonstration is throughout all space and all time (Eph. 3:20–21).

Repeating, none of these things are said by God of any other institution.

Now, in these days the church may seem to us a ragtag affair without much rhyme or reason. That's because we're looking at the tapestry on the wrong side, with all its yarn ends showing. Just wait till eternity and we'll see the church on the other side, where God sees it! Oh, glory! Dazzling brilliance and splendor!

Don't bad-mouth the church, my friend. Don't put any activity or group, not even any parachurch movement, above the church. The church is Christ's Body.

Now, I understand that there's a difference between the visible church and the invisible. I know that the local "First Church" on the corner downtown is probably a mixture of true believers and fakes. But precisely because we don't have the eyes to see which is which, we'd better treat the whole visible church with some kind of respect!

A few years ago the battles were hot between this Council and that, and we had our guns trained on what might have been our brothers, instead of on Satan, our true enemy. God's angel will one day sickle out the tares from the wheat, but in the meantime, let's be careful how we handle even the visible church. You may not decide to attend a certain one, but you don't have to take potshots at it.

Think about how Christ identifies with the church. Here was Paul, on the road to Damascus. He thought he'd only been giving *Christians* a hard time, but when he said, "Who art thou, Lord?" Jesus answered, "I am Jesus, *whom you are persecuting.*"

To persecute a brother is to persecute Jesus. To speak roughly of a brother is to speak roughly of Jesus. To touch his disciple is to touch him! (Ray's comment on this once when he was preaching: "We say we want to learn to worship here at Lake Avenue Church. We won't learn worship until we learn unity. When we treat the Lord's people with tenderness and reverence, we adore him, worship him, treat him well, too!")

So how do we act out that the church is such a high, precious priority in our lives, second only to the Lord himself, who is mystically part of it—the most important part? At that particular conference I suggested four ways:

1. By guarding and handling with care our oneness. That's what Ephesians 4:2, 3 tells us to do: with complete humility and gentleness and patience, "make every effort to keep the unity of the Spirit through the bond of peace." Dietrich Bonhoeffer saw a great truth when he said that our fellowship is not based on how godly the other Christian is, but it's based on what Christ has done for both of us.

Acts 2:4 says that all the believers were filled with the Holy Spirit. That is totally unifying. There is nothing exclusive or discriminatory about it.

When we share the Spirit of Christ and concentrate on him, differences shrink down, or melt away. If we settle into secondary things, we'll bicker and argue: if we're occupied, for instance, with details of the regulations we set for our lifestyles; or with liturgies, ceremonies, and church customs; or with secondary doctrinal issues; or with affairs of government, political parties, national issues, and so on.

We're drawn and held together by the Spirit on the basics: God, sin, death, sacrifice, love. We must stay solidly on the basics to maintain unity and sweetness.

Recently Ray and Nels and I sat on some grass and listened to a beautiful symphony orchestra. Hundreds of us, probably greatly diverse in our lives and philosophies, were caught up into the same beauty. So Christians must minimize differences and be caught up together in the beauty of Jesus Christ.

And how do we act out that the church is such a precious, high priority?

2. By repairing any rift that comes along in the body (Eph. 4:31-32).

Have you ever been sad over the split of those former partners, Barnabas and Paul, in Acts 15:39-40? You remember the story. Paul and Barnabas were traveling and preaching, and picked up Barnabas's cousin John Mark (Col. 4:10) to go along with them. Later when the going got rough, Mark deserted. Barnabas could forgive him and later wanted to sign him up again, but Paul said "nothing doing." And the debate got so hot that Barnabas took Mark and went off to preach, and Paul took a new partner, Silas (Acts 15:36-41).

Barnabas had been wonderful from Acts 4:36 on. What happened that he lost his head? After the fight we never hear of him again, unless it's that sad little note about him in Galatians 2:13.

The issue wasn't doctrine but personality. The issue wasn't

who was right. I suppose, actually, Paul was the rigid one—he was so dedicated, he couldn't stand for Barnabas's relative Mark to be less dedicated. Our little saying, "If Christ is not Lord of all, he is not Lord at all" can make us too tough and unforgiving and critical, can't it! (Acknowledging Christ's "Lordship" is a growing commitment to Christ.)

It's not easy to be a member of the family of God. You can't have close relationships without occasionally getting hurt, just the way you do in a physical family. But be careful not to get to be a fussy, divisive, critical Christian!

Even our profound convictions, my friend, are not infallible. Let's leave room for others' convictions, even though we remain true to our own. Unity is so precious, it must be highly prized, sought after, and maintained!

3. By accepting each other as we are (Eph. 5:1–2). The loving church has a wonderful fragrance about it. Love each other—period!—not because of worth!

Gilbert Tennant was a Presbyterian pastor in Philadelphia in 1750, during the days of the "Great Awakening." In a Lake Avenue Church sermon, Ray describes one of Tennant's sermons like this:

> He urged his congregation to love each other, and love each other to the end. He said when you begin to love each other you come to a certain place—oh, hear me, my friends!—you come at a certain place when you discover the real truth.
>
> And in every one of our lives there's a can of worms. Believe you me! There's a skeleton in the closet of every life here. And you see, we can be willing to be known, or we can be willing to know, up to that point. That's it.
>
> That's safe, but that's superficial. But, [Tennant] says, you must love right in through that painful area, . . . love right on to the end. Refuse to let go, though you know everything about that person. Refuse to let go!
>
> . . . Fragile love will love up to a point, and that's not worth

anything. That's what most Christians experience. But there are those who are willing to know and willing to be known to the point where they go crashing right on through that threshhold of pain—to where they really know and are known!

There's a bumper sticker I see sometimes on the backs of cars that says, "Christians aren't perfect; they're just forgiven."

4. By adapting and fitting in with each other (Eph. 5:21). It's so important to become interdependent! Have you thought it was strange that the Macedonians first gave themselves to God, and then to Paul and company (2 Cor. 8:5)? Well, Paul had done it, too: the first thing he did after he gave himself to Christ was submit to other Christians (Acts 22:10–16).

Everybody in God's family is to submit to everybody else. That's what makes it hot in there; it takes courage to plunge into the life of the Body. We can't be loners any more. We can't do what we want to do, when we want to do it. "Well," says a Christian willing to take the plunge, *"C'est la vie."*

And he turns out to be *right!* That's life! That's real living—gutsy, dangerous, thrilling, scary, exhausting, rewarding!

It's the only way to live. It's God's way.

5.

Getting Our Loving Right Side Up

Oh, oh. I'm going to be in trouble in this chapter. Help me, Lord Jesus Christ, to say it right. Help the readers to "hang in" with me to the end, to get the whole picture. Help us all to see your truth.

Here we go.

I have a conviction that we haven't started to function too well yet with each other as Christians because we haven't seen the difference between dust and stars.

Back in Genesis 13:16, when Abraham had chosen his land and decided to settle in it, God said to him, "Abram, I will make your descendants as the dust of the earth." Following an "earthly" decision, God gave him a fabulous promise about his future family: they'd be as plentiful as "earthly" dust.

In Genesis 15:6 Abraham "believed the Lord, and he credited it to him as righteousness," a foundation verse on which all the remainder of "faith teaching" in the Bible rests. And in connection with it, God said, "Abram, your descendants will be as plentiful as the stars."

God repeated the double promise in Genesis 22:17: "I will surely bless you and make your descendants as numerous as the stars in the sky and as the sand on the seashore."

Let's "spiritualize" for a moment God's beautiful analogy of dust and stars. Romans 4:11-18—as well as other places in the New Testament—spells out how God's double promise resulted in a double line of descendants: the Jews, Abraham's earthly descendants by physical heritage, as numerous as dust; and all the believers, Abraham's heavenly descendants by spiritual heritage, as numerous as stars. Abraham had two great families.

Unless we keep these families separate, we get into all kinds of problems. The beautiful thing we have in common is the same father, Abraham!

The whole Old Testament is a story of the development of Abraham's physical descendants, the Jews. Their family structure was strictly physical. They were born into their immediate family, and into a certain clan with a common paternal ancestor, and the clan within one of the tribes, all descended from twelve brothers, and the tribe within the nation Israel, all physically related. In that setup the physical father was also the spiritual head of the home. He was answerable for the sins and successes of the mother and the children; he provided the information for census-taking; he was responsible to teach them and lead them in all things, including spiritual things.

The New Testament, or Covenant, is really new! It brings in a new order. And "by calling this covenant 'new,' he has made the first one obsolete" (Heb. 8:13a). It's the story of Abraham's spiritual descendants—those who have believed in God's Son Jesus Christ, and God counts it to them as righteousness, as he did their spiritual father Abraham. There are no physical fathers, clans, or tribes here. No one is born into it by natural birth; we must be "born again" into it, because it's a spiritual family.

The differences between the Old and New Testaments are

striking. Even meanings for identical words change.

The word *family* is used around 200 times in the Old Testament, and it always means physical family. But in the New Testament? Well, Luke 2:4, still in the culture of the Old Testament and of the law, uses the word *family* meaning "physical family" for the last time in the Bible, saying that Joseph "was of the house and family of David" (NASB).[1] After that it's gone.

The word *family* does appear twice more, in Acts 3:25 and in Ephesians 3:15—first, meaning mankind in general ("all the families of the earth")[2] and then, even broader, "whole family in heaven and on earth."[3]

Certainly you can say that from the cross on, physical families are never mentioned in the Bible: "households," yes—including servants, houseguests, anybody under a single roof—but never physical families in the strict sense that the Old Testament had used the word.

The word *father* is used around 600 times in the Old Testament, and it practically always means physical father. Seven times God is poetically called "father" (Jer. 3:4, 19; 31:9; Deut. 32:6; Isa. 63:16; 64:8; Mal. 1:6), but the Israelites didn't really think of him that way. On the other hand, the word *father* occurs about 300 times in the New Testament, and it almost always means God. It was a wonderful new concept of him!

Brother occurs around 120 times in the Old Testament and meant physical brother. It occurs nearly 100 times in the New Testament and nearly always means "brother in Christ." *Children* in the Old Testament meant physical offspring. In the New, it takes on the tender meaning of spiritual children, as in Ephesians 5:1 and all the endearments in 1 John.

The New Testament is definitely a family book, but it's the

spiritual family that comes into prominence—which is newer, higher, and eternal!

Jesus' life is the pivotal hinge between Old and New Testaments, because he came to introduce the world to concepts they'd never thought of under the law. Certainly he supported that precious, God-given physical family: he defended the sanctity of marriage (Mark 10:9) and he rebuked the Pharisees for avoiding taking care of aging parents (Mark 7:10–13).

But Jesus was introducing a higher order of family life than had ever been thought of—one we really have not yet comprehended, but now perhaps the time has come!

Prayerfully look at what the Gospels say. First we see Jesus when he was twelve. Found by his parents—after much searching—in the temple, he was rebuked by his mother: "Son, why have you treated us like this? Your father and I have been anxiously searching for you." His answer put them at a little distance: "Why were you searching for me? Didn't you know I had to be in my father's house?" And Luke says "they did not understand what he was saying to them" (Luke 2:48–50). No, their Old Testament minds knew only one kind of father—like Joseph.

The very next verse says that he was still subject to his parents at that age, and yet he had already demonstrated in his thinking some higher kind of priority than he could give to an earthly father and mother.

Now the Scriptures are going to get hotter to handle. Remember that Jesus always taught in a powerful, revolutionary way. We don't seem to mind, if it only hit the Pharisees' pet ideas; we just don't want him to hit ours! But to teach higher truths about the new spiritual family emerging, Jesus taught by contrast, and he said it more strongly than you or I would ever dare, or even think appropriate.

In Matthew and Luke he says he was come to set members of physical families against each other, and that anyone who loves his father or mother or his son or daughter "more than me is not worthy of me" (Matt. 10:34–37). In Luke 14 he says it even more daringly: "If anyone comes to me and does not hate his father and mother, his wife and children, his brothers and sisters—yes, even his own life—he cannot be my disciple" (Luke 14:26).

What on earth can these words mean? The one who said them is Love personified! Let's stick together to the end of the next two chapters.

Look at Jesus' personal example, with his own physical family. After his first recorded rebuff as a twelve-year-old, we see him next confronting his mother at his first public miracle, and he says to her, "Dear woman, why do you involve me?" Well, we know he wasn't angry at her because immediately afterward, they went home together (John 2:4, 12).

But soon, when he's preaching, someone calls out from the crowd, "Blessed is the mother who gave you birth and nursed you." He could have just smiled and nodded and gone on with his sermon, but he calls back, "Blessed rather are those who hear the Word of God and obey it" (Luke 11:27–28). Ouch! How did I get into this? But at least, through the fog, we see that our all-wise, all-loving Lord Jesus Christ seemed to be giving priority to his spiritual family over his physical family.

And look what we have next: Jesus is preaching again and someone says to him, "Your mother and your brothers are standing outside wanting to speak to you."

He replied, "Who is my mother, and who are my brothers?" Pointing to his disciples, he said, "Here are my mother and my brothers. For whoever does the will of my Father [catch that relationship, too] in heaven is my brother and sister and mother" (Matt. 12:47–50).

Why do we have these rebuffs? Why does Jesus seem to deliberately give attention to his spiritual family at the expense of his physical family?

I think of two possible reasons. One, because his time was short, and he had to pour everything he could into strengthening the believers—and particularly the twelve apostles, who would be the foundation pillars of the whole church to follow.

And two, because he loves his especially chosen, God-given physical family so deeply that he knew a lifestyle of total obedience to God was the only way ultimately to win them! They didn't need his time for time's sake—sitting home playing tiddly-winks in the sunshine of Nazareth in order to prove himself a good "brother and son" of the family. They needed to see a life lived wholly for God, and that would be the power they finally couldn't resist!

They did resist for a long time. Mark 3:21 and John 7:5 tell us that during his three years of ministry, they didn't believe in him. That must have given him great pangs of loneliness and sadness. But eventually, his unswerving, visible godliness won their hearts!

Look who was in the "upper room" following his ascension, praying and waiting for Pentecost: "They all joined together constantly in prayer, along with the women and Mary the mother of Jesus, and his brothers" (Acts 1:14).

Yea! Hooray! Three cheers! Throw up your hats! When the time finally came to be counted, there they were!

And look who became traveling preachers, going everywhere with the new Gospel of Jesus Christ! Paul wrote: "Don't we have the right to take a believing wife along with us [when we travel and preach], as do the Lord's brothers?" (1 Cor. 9:5).

How about that! The power of the life of a physical Brother, Jesus, who gave himself to God as his highest priority and then to his spiritual family in all of those meaningful and eternally important interactions—that power was finally irresistible, and the physical brothers, too, reached for what they saw in him.

And look who wrote two Holy Spirit-directed letters which became part of the Word of God: two of the brothers, James and Jude (Matt. 13:55). It must have been a final, wonderful triumph for Jesus to see his own precious physical family become greatly used by God!

Think about Jesus' mother, too. She'd been told thirty years before by the prophet Simon that "a sword will pierce your own soul" (Luke 2:35). When her son was dying on the cross, you'd think that would have been the sword piercing her, but Jesus' words must even have given the sword a twist. He said, "Dear woman, here is your son!" and to John standing by, "Here is your mother!" (John 19:26–27). He was actually making the final break in the physical relationship between them!

Why was Jesus turning his mother over to a new son? Dr. Russell Bradley Jones says,

> The word that grieved Mary so when it was spoken proved, by time's interpretation, to be a blessed word indeed. Mary discovered that she had been led from a natural union *with Jesus* to a mystical union *with Christ*. She gladly took her place among his sincere worshippers. It was not a special place, it was not on a platform; it was with the 120, as a simple believer!
>
> She found that the salvation relationship is higher than the family relationship. She learned that it was better to have him as her Saviour and Lord than to have him as her son.

And in a very true sense, she discovered that her former son had made better provision for her as her Saviour than he could have made as her son. Heavenly mansions and eternal life are hardly to be compared with a few fleeting years in John's [home]! [4]

Now let's look at the disciples. They had to follow the example of Jesus, and it must have really seemed painful for the moment.

Take Peter, for example. We know he had a home and a wife and a mother-in-law (Luke 4:38). Biblical scholars tell us that the first half of Jesus' ministry, the Twelve probably still lived at home and only joined him on public occasions. But there came that last year and a half when the Twelve went "on the road" with him, and that must have seemed tough and maybe even unreasonable. We might tend to think today with our twisted priorities that it just wouldn't be *spiritual* for Jesus to call a man to leave his family to serve him—even for roughly eighteen months!

Peter, feeling this deeply at one point, commented, "We have left all we had to follow you!"

"I tell you the truth," Jesus said to them, "no one who has left home or wife or brothers or parents or children for the sake of the kingdom of God will fail to receive many times as much in this age and, in the age to come, eternal life" (Luke 18:28–30).

The promise here is for the exchange of physical family for spiritual family; of a few, for multitudes; of a temporary family for an eternal one; of a family which may inherit a few dollars in the bank for co-heirs with Jesus Christ of all God's glory. Maybe at the moment that didn't seem like much of an exchange to Peter. But he was willing to be obedient, and after a few months' separation, God gave him back a wife who was a new sister in Christ and who was constantly at his side in his preaching and traveling! (1 Cor. 9:5).

What would Peter have missed, if he'd put his wife first and refused? Remember the fellow in Jesus' parable who rejected the invitation to dinner because he said, "I just got married, so I can't come"? Jesus said, "I tell you, not one of those men who were invited will get a taste of my banquet" (Luke 14: 20, 24). We shudder to think of all Peter would have lost—and Peter's wife, too.

Now, after Jesus' life, which was the transition period between the old family and the new, the new was actually born: the church, the *ecclesia,* which means "the called-out ones."

And so they are. Here's a street of typical family homes. Under one roof two are called-out ones, and three are not. Under the next three roofs there are no believers. Then under the next roof there is one who is called out. And down the block, praise God, there's a whole family of Christians. But if you were to draw a diagram of that street, all of those called-out ones would meet together over the rooftops in a glorious, eternity-destined spiritual family.

As we begin to see things in proportion, we see no putdown of the physical family in God's economy. (The human family is God's own fabulous invention, and it is far more precious to him than it is even to us. Never must we forget that.) But we see an even higher, more glorious order: the newly created (but eternally predestined) spiritual family. He is not lowering the physical; he is only elevating the spiritual. And oh, how we need a vision of that elevation!

Look at the conversion of Saul, soon after the birth of the spiritual family. He meets Jesus on the road to Damascus, is "born again," and three days later meets Ananias, who lays hands on him and says "Brother Saul" (Acts 9:17). *Brother*—? How strange, how tender, how new! It must have warmed him, and made his heart beat faster. Unless Saul had physical brothers, probably no one had ever called him that before. And it meant so much to him that when he retold the story of his conversion, he repeated what Ananias had called him (Acts 22:13).

From here on the message was, "Everyone who calls upon the name of the Lord will be saved." And whether they came by ones or by twos or by fives, they became part of a wonderful, new, eternal family—of spiritual aunts and uncles and grandparents and sons and fathers!

Here was Timothy, a young man with a grandmother and a mother who were believers (2 Tim. 1:5), but a father who apparently was not (Acts 16:1). Are we going to say, "Poor Timothy! He'll never amount to much; he didn't have a good father-image"? (How sad when we think first in terms of the physical family!) Paul took him right to his side as his son and became his spiritual father (1 Tim. 1:2). He had him circumcised; he kept him beside him on trips; he called him "my son" and discipled him; and when Paul himself faded off the scene, Timothy was one of the leading lights of the early church.

Timothy's physical father may have been a spiritual loser; we don't know. If he was, that was his own decision. We hope eventually he was converted, but there's no record of it. But Timothy was not grievously injured, because when he was taken into that glorious spiritual family—the purpose of that family is to heal all the hurts and fill in all the lacks created by the imperfect physical family, and to turn out whole people—better able to love their physical families than ever before.

And Paul didn't just function only as a father. He was brother to spiritual sisters like Phoebe (Rom. 16:1) and men like Epaphroditus (Phil. 2:25), and he was like a son to Rufus' mother, who he said was a spiritual mother to him (Rom. 16:13).

We have many roles to play, and we must learn to play them all. Ray and I loved it when our older son Bud wrote us from college and called us "sister mother" and "brother dad"! Right on!

1 Timothy 5:1–2 tells us: "Do not rebuke an older man harshly, but exhort him as if he were your father. Treat younger men as brothers, older women as mothers, and younger women as sisters, with absolute purity."

We've learned a lot in recent years about the church's being the Body of Christ, and, thinking about hands and feet and eyes and mouths, we've sought to discover our gifts and function with them. That's one picture of the church, and a wonderful one, and we praise God for this rediscovery of truth.

But that concept isn't all. If we know only this kind of "Body" life, we've left lots of single adults standing awkwardly around the scene without family. We have numberless teenagers from non-Christian homes who have no spiritual parents to guide them and who get all their wisdom from their own peers in the youth group—poor Timothys without Pauls! We have lonely widows and widowers, and other former wives and husbands floating around like second-class citizens—because we tend to think mostly "physical family," and to make our churches couples-oriented and physical-family–oriented.

Maybe what we're doing is functioning like dust instead of stars! We could be trying to force the New Testament scene to fit the Old Testament pattern of fathers, families, clans, and tribes. If we are—hooray, then, for the rare and lucky physical families who fit the bill, whose members can all answer to the spiritual roll call, too. We gear our churches to meet their needs.

But that's not the *"ecclesia"!* The called-out ones come from every possible broken-family situation; and not until we see ourselves as functioning first as a spiritual family will we all draw together and meet each others' needs.

We can't organize this; but we must teach it and learn it well, and then let the Holy Spirit make it happen. It comes out of a deep understanding of "priority two" [5]—and a deep commitment to each other, our beautiful forever-family of God.

6.

The Ultimate Family

Don't make up your mind too quickly on what we're talking about. I do believe when Jesus, love's Creator and Love itself, talked about "hating" physical family, it must have been for the sake of contrast. Rather than "putting down" the precious physical family he'd created, he was lifting up new relationships in such a forceful way that we'd never forget it!

Nobody ever had a more beautiful physical family than I've had, either my past one, or my present.

Daddy was orphaned very young, and struggled up through such amazing circumstances that I'd love to write a book about him; and he had a distinguished career as a U.S. Army officer, the last years as a Brigadier General. Mother was his lady, and lady she was.

My earliest memories of them are when Daddy was tall, athletic, fun, and greying in his early thirties, one of the Army's outstanding polo players; and Mother was slender and willowy with big, dark eyes and masses of dark hair. I got to eat the crusts the maid cut off the sandwiches before afternoon bridge groups came to our quarters. And on Saturdays my brother Bobby and I would join all the rest of the post kids in matinees of Charlie Chaplin and Harold Lloyd, while Daddy and Mother went off riding together in their jodhpurs and boots. Saturday nights we kissed them goodbye when they went off to the post dances—Daddy so erect and proud in his dress blues, and Mother smelling delicious, sometimes in an evening dress of chiffon with huge purple and rose tulips. Wow! Then Julia would tuck Bobby and me into bed.

Then Daddy and Mother started attending a post Bible class for officers and wives taught by a Col. and Mrs. Titus, and they met Jesus Christ in new, living, fresh ways. The revolution was so total that for the next forty years they, too, taught Bible classes on all the posts where Daddy was ever stationed, and they led literally hundreds of officers and wives to know Jesus Christ. The same personal stature that had charmed others in their lives "B.C.," now was used by the Lord to make them great spiritual leaders.

The transformation didn't mean less fun or attention for us kids. Bobby and I were joined by sisters Mary Alice and Margie, and we grew up with great memories of our family of six. There were lots of family picnics and outings. Post chapels never had any Sunday evening services, so Sunday nights were family game times, in the winter in front of the fire. Out came the bridge table for Rook, Bunco, Muggins, Lindy, Parcheesi, and lots more, with toasted sandwiches and cocoa in a blue Japanese teapot with a broken nose.

Mother eventually bowed out of riding, but for years Daddy took us kids cross-country every Saturday in our jodhpurs and boots; and Bobby, when he was a teenager, owned his own horse. Daddy and Mother sang a lot together—including a lot of silly old college songs from their courting days, and everybody took piano lessons and later pipe organ.

And forty years later? Mother and Daddy went to heaven

just about the same time, three years ago. They were buried in Arlington Cemetery next to Bobby, a fervent Christian Air Force pilot whose plane went down in World War II when he was twenty-four, and when his twin sons were three weeks old. Both twins strongly identify with the dad they never knew: one, Joe Sweet, who bears his general-grandfather's name, is a minister now; and the other is the second Captain Bob Sweet, U.S. Air Force—and also flying for the Lord.

Mary Alice is married to an elder of the Fourth Presbyterian Church in Washington, D.C., where Dick Halverson is pastor, and their two children are outstanding. One has a fine Christian wife, and the other is overseas in temporary missionary service.

Sister Margie is married to the pastor of the North Avenue Presbyterian Church in Atlanta, and their five beautiful children, kindergarten through teenage, all love the Lord.

And my immediate family? My Ray is pastor of the Lake Avenue Congregational Church in Pasadena, California. Our oldest daughter, Sherry, is married to a seminary graduate who sings for the Lord as first tenor on the "Haven of Rest" radio broadcast. Our other daughter, Margie, is married to a pastor, and our older son, Bud, is a pastor, and all of their children who have reached the "age of accountability" have accepted Christ. Nels, our thirteen-year-old, loves him, too.

Not counting the babies, the other twenty-eight would tell you that the grandparents have had a remarkable effect on their lives and hearts and memories. And there's not a rebel in the lot, nor a divorce, nor amazingly, even any ill health.

So I know, truly, what it is to be wrapped up in the security of a good "physical family." And how God loves that, too! He started off the human race with a family; the family was his idea of how to incorporate tenderness and responsibility and discipling and all the rest into the human scene.

When Adam's descendants fell into gross sin, God brought the flood and then started in again with a new family: Noah, his wife, their three sons and their wives.

And when Noah's descendants defiantly built the tower of Babel, God scattered them all and started with a new family: Abraham and his generations. This Jewish race was his most spectacular and most visible family, with the most care built in for their spiritual and physical preservation, through the giving of the Law.

But when even that "Exhibit A" of the family failed, Christ came along with strong words to say, "Don't pin all your hopes on the physical family. I won't destroy it by any means. I will continue to affirm it and use it, but I'll superimpose upon it a mystical, eternal, spiritual family who will be my very own true family at last—the one I've been waiting for. My own Father will call himself their Father, also, and they will be his children. And although I am his divine Son, I will not be ashamed to call them 'brothers' (Heb. 2:11–12), and the family spirit with which I'll endue them will be Our own all-Holy Spirit. Their inheritance will not be just physical property; I promise them every spiritual blessing in heavenly places (Eph. 1:3). My strongest word to them will be unity; but after their poor, dear, bungling attempts at relationships on earth, We the Trinity will make them one forever in glory, in just the same way that We the Godhead are one!" (John 17:11).

And so Jesus spelled out the beginnings of the new family plan. When he taught them to pray, he said, "Our Father ..."! (Matt. 6:9). How the listeners' ears must have tingled! It was an almost unknown concept to think of God in that close, personal way.

Through Jesus' ministry he referred over and over to God as his own heavenly Father, but what a remarkable thing he said to Mary after his resurrection: "Go to my *brothers* and say to them, 'I ascend to *my Father* and *your Father*, and my God and your God'" (John 20:17). He spelled it out for emphasis.

And Romans 8:15 reaches the highest, sweetest pinnacle of it all when it says we're even allowed to cry out, "Abba"— "Daddy!"—"Papa!" It's so wonderful, it's almost too much. Even today little Middle Eastern children run out of their tents or houses to meet Daddy, crying, "Abba! Abba! Abba!" It's a name so easy to say, it's one of the first baby words. To say "Abba" you don't even need any teeth!

What a long, long way we've come. In the Old Testament, Daddy was Daddy. Hopefully, you obeyed him, but also, his knees could be hugged, his hair could be pulled, and his cheek could be pinched. But God? His name wasn't even pronounceable: it was the Tetragrammaton, "I AM," with four consonants and no vowels. Hopefully, you obeyed him, because if you didn't, there was eternal judgment. But call him by a family name? Oh, no.

Jeremy Taylor said it so well:

> He hath changed the ineffable Name into a Name utterable by man, and desirable by all the world; the Majesty is arrayed in robes of mercy, the Tetragrammaton or Adorable Mystery of the patriarchs is made fit for pronunciation and expression when it becometh the Name of the Lord's Christ.

Praise him! Alleluia! Don't ever take for granted how wonderful it is to have God as your Father—your very own "Abba"! Oh, no matter how limited your physical father was, you're not cheated; you don't have to be stunted. You have the best of all possible fathers. You have *The Father!*

Don't forget, to repeat, that Jesus never undermined the underpinnings of the physical family: he defended the holiness of marriage, and he emphasized the absolute urgency of material care, especially the care of older parents (Mark 7:10–13). How consistent the New Testament is! Jesus himself arranged care for his own mother when he was gone (John 19:26–27). And 1 Timothy 5:4 repeats the same instructions about being financially responsible for parents, and goes on to make the matter absolutely clear: "If any one does not provide for his own, and especially those of his own household, he has denied the faith and is worse than an unbeliever" (1 Tim. 5:8).

Wow! You just can't get any stronger than that. It's as "hot under the collar" as Jesus' words when chiding them for the same thing—not paying parents' bills. He said, "Hypocrites! ...[God says] 'In vain you worship me'" (Mark 7:6–7).

And this isn't just some weight around the necks of the men. Women are just as responsible if they're able, according to 1 Timothy 5:16.

The New Testament certainly infers important things about physical families. It says that those given, social relationships are a starting point for learning how to behave with each other. A "household" consisted of those under the same roof, including servants. I would think today it would also mean college dorm roommates, singles sharing an apartment, and so on. These "households" are the lab in which relationships can be purified in obedience to God.

But in the three places in the New Testament where the physical family is talked about at some length, the social institutions are lumped together: husband-wife relationships, parent-child, and master-slave (1 Cor. 7; Eph. 5:22–6:9; Col.

3:18–25). None of these relationships is given as God's highest order for humans on earth. These verses simply say, "You're probably already in one or more of these relationships; behave within them in Christ-like ways."

Certainly all of us are painfully aware of the shaky state of the physical family in the world today. God has loved the physical family ever since he invented it in the Garden of Eden. He has defended it. He has given it status. He has made it one of the great underpinnings of society, just as government is an underpinning. In the last days before Christ's return society will be greatly undermined because, among other things, men will "despise authorities" (2 Pet. 2:10) and be "disobedient to parents" (2 Tim. 3:2).

Christians must be careful not to "bad-mouth" social institutions. God has given these as anchors and stabilizers for rebellious societies. We must submit to our governments, pray for our leaders, and teach our children to respect laws and authorities (Rom. 13:1–7).

And we must zealously protect and defend the physical family! It also is God's glue to hold society together. Marriage is sacred. Parents must be obeyed. More than other families, especially Christian families must be shored up and encouraged in every possible way.

And the relationship of husband and wife is a picture of that of God with Israel, or of Christ with the church. What a precious earthly relationship! No wonder God hates divorce (Mal. 2:16).

Still, no Christian single adult needs to think he's missing some great spiritual "thing" because he's not a part of this heavenly representation on earth. He is—not represents, but actually is—not Christ's wife, but his very Body! Do you see it? Do you catch the difference? There is no higher privilege.

Now, when we consider the weakened condition of the physical family today, we thank the Lord for all the books, seminars, and any other teaching aids to help it. However, does it seem that with all our aids, the family is still shakier than it ought to be? Could it be that the Body of Christ has not learned to function very well as a spiritual family first of all, and that's why Christians are so unsupported that they can't perform very well at home?

There is far more in the New Testament on how to function within the spiritual family than within the physical. God had to write it this way for a reason. The brothers and sisters are to love each other "with all purity" and yet all familial tenderness. The older men are to be surrogate fathers where needed, and the older women, extra mothers to the younger women (Tit. 2:3-5). Surely if we Christians did these things well, the church would be full of living models to teach how to be physical spouses, parents, daughters and sons at home.

Oh, all of us who are children of God! How untaught we are in how to treat each other! How distracted we are by our lonely pursuits! How numb we are to each others' private pain! How totally desperate some of us are to know and to be known—to have someone, or just a few, who really care!

What do strangers look for in a new church? They want one that's "friendly." So the pastor tries to get his people to smile and shake hands with visitors, but it's not easy. They hardly do it to each other; why should they with someone they don't know? And so most Christianity turns out seeming so anesthetized, so cold, so drugged—as if it's about to sink down into the snows of death.

This book is a shout, a scream, a call: Fuse, brothers, fuse! Put away whatever is dividing you! Sign a pact with your blood! Place yourselves deeply, deeply together—whatever its awkwardness or pain!

Reach anew to God, then reach to each other. Only then can you reach out to the world.

(Oops. I broke my pencil point. Whenever I begin to feel something really deeply, and feel that you should feel it, too— I get writing faster and faster and crying as I write—and I break my point. End of chapter.)

7.

What Will Help That Precious Physical Family?

I've been assigned the specific role of temporary mother to two kids: a white boy and a black girl.

Cathy was in one of my small groups, and her high school son was keeping his distance. "Cathy," I said, "let me lend a hand in mothering your child." We both knew this may be a part of putting our lives together, to be available to each others' kids. When Jonathan and David made a covenant of friendship, it was to include responsibility for their children (1 Sam. 20:15–16; 2 Sam. 9).

I invited Cathy's son out for a coke date. Wonder of wonders, he accepted! Over the weeks we shared our lives together, and I poured out some of my troubles to him, and he poured out to me his girlfriend troubles, his parent troubles, his frustrations. We giggled together, and we talked seriously together. After a few months, with no pushing from me, he'd decided his girl was the wrong one for him (he was right), and he was praying out loud with me, and he'd rejoined the church youth group to make some new friends. When his mother reported he was hugging her in the kitchen, I knew my job was over.

Patty was the daughter of another of my dear friends, and

Patty was going through the inevitable confusion, as a black high schooler in a mostly white church, of finding out who she was. Oh, how my heart went out to her—so beautiful, and with so much potential.

Some of our coke dates were stormy. "Patty," I told her once, "you're the most selfish person I know!" (God help me! She really had to put up with a lot.) "There are plenty of dear brothers and sisters in Lake Avenue Church who are facing old age, or who've discovered they have cancer, or who have unbelievably hard marriages, and you don't know about any of them. You're just aware of yourself because you happen to be black!"

Poor Patty! I was too dumb to realize that any high school age child is aware only of himself, because that's the way it is at that time of life. She was good to stick with me.

I have a lunch date with Patty coming up. By now she's a grown, poised, glamorous woman launched into a career, and what turns her on most of all is Jesus, and praising him, and witnessing of him. I'm honored to be her friend.

Our own children certainly have had plenty of extra parents, too. Ray and I are not smart enough to be "all in all" to them; that puts too much pressure on us. We love them the most, and we do all we can, and they know they finally answer to us; but along the way we also expose them to all the godly adults possible.

Our son Nels can't receive everything he needs from one set of parents. He's richer for having hundreds! And I remember when our older three got into the teen years, how comforting it was to Ray and me that when they were at the time of being weaned away emotionally from us, other godly adults were saying what we would have said, in fresh words.

Praise the Lord for Leta Fischer! Hundreds of teenagers

called her "Mother Fischer" for years. Our two daughters poured out to her all the boyfriend woes that we knew nothing about, and she cried with them, quoted poetry to them, recited Scripture verses by the dozens, and helped steer them through the tough years. Meanwhile, Bud, our son, had Glen Dawson and Larry Harter and other extra fathers.

Now Bud and our daughters are our best friends again, but in the growing-out-of-the-nest period, when it was essential for them to get emotionally disentangled from us, their physical parents, it was crucial to have spiritual parents who guided them in the same direction and made the transition smooth.

If the Ortlund family, all together in Christ, needs the larger spiritual family to help us, surely those from broken physical families do, too.

I've watched dear Fran since the days when she was a pastor's wife with small children, through the years when her husband left her and she returned to settle back into Lake Avenue Church and steer her children through their teens. Fran tells me they never would have made it, and neither would she, without church men who've befriended her kids and provided the good "father-image" they needed.

Evon is our church's head usher, and he's such a gentle, gracious encourager of people—a true Barnabas! A while back, Evon stooped over to talk to a little girl.

"I'm a grandpa," said Evon. "Do you have a grandpa?"

"No," said the little girl, and her father hastened to explain that both her grandparents had passed away.

"Well," said Evon, "I'll be your grandpa."

And that was the start of a tender new relationship. Evon and his wife have been in their house. They've been to his. That little girl has a new grandpa, and she can grow up with grandpa-memories being built into her life. And I don't know what her other grandpas were like—probably they were wonderful men; but I do know this grandpa will minister Jesus to her over the years.

The stories I've told aren't to say that every church should now post new relationships up on their bulletin boards in some kind of structured new program. But if we believers will get the picture of how we're to function as God's beautiful "ultimate family," the Holy Spirit will do the rest—day by day, as opportunities arise!

When Jesus promised Peter a hundred times as many mothers, fathers, brothers, sisters, sons, and daughters as he had ever given up, he was looking toward a rich new family that would satisfy Peter's needs better than his "household" family ever could. (And remember the *substitution* lasted only roughly a year and a half. Mostly, the spiritual family was *in addition to* —a double blessing.)

Think about it. Because of the support and input of his physical family, Peter had grown to be a mature professional fisherman with undoubtedly a sense of responsibility and many other fine qualities. Praise God for his provision of physical families, with all that nurture and support and stimulus they provide! They are the springboard for great attainment in this world.

But think of the input of Jesus and the other disciples for three years on Peter, and then the thrill of representing the Twelve in preaching on the day of Pentecost (Acts 2:14). Think of the stimulus Cornelius provided, showing Peter that the whole Gentile world was waiting to be opened up for the Gospel (Acts 10). What about when he got thrown into prison, and all the brothers and sisters had an all-night prayer meeting for him? (Acts 12). How about the "tough love" Paul showed Peter when he rebuked him to his face, one time when he turned hypocrite? (Gal. 2:11–14). Or the awesome thrill of being considered at last one of the three pillars of the mother church in Jerusalem? (Gal. 2:9).

Over the years Peter was so intellectually and spiritually and emotionally stimulated and motivated by spiritual brothers, sisters, parents, and children, that he wrote two of our greatest pieces of literature. Imagine a fisherman from up-country Galilee writing like this about silver, seed, and stars:

> You were not redeemed with perishable things like silver or gold from your futile way of life inherited from your forefathers, but with precious blood, as of a lamb unblemished and spotless, the blood of Christ (1 Pet. 1:18–19).
>
> You have been born again not of seed which is perishable but imperishable, that is, through the living and abiding Word of God (1 Pet. 1:23).
>
> So we have the prophetic word made more sure, to which you do well to pay attention as to a lamp shining in a dark place, until the day dawns, and the morning star arises in your hearts (2 Pet. 1:19).

How awed, amazed, and thrilled Peter's wife must have been to hear her ex-fisherman husband preach like that, and to read his writings! And she knew *she* hadn't stimulated all that in him—nor had his parents back in Galilee. I feel the same way about Ray. I can't clutch at him; I have to turn him loose. Fabulous things happen between him and dozens of his brothers and sisters in Christ; their imprint on him is as wonderful as his on them; and then he's vastly richer when he comes back to me. Indeed, a far more wonderful husband and father!

How many problems in the physical family would be solved or at least alleviated if the spiritual family were really functioning?

Let me quote from my book *Disciplines of the Beautiful Woman:*

A deep prayer life with, and accountability to, some close members of the spiritual family can help make your relationship with your physical family what it ought to be.

There's a lot of talk these days which pits the church against the family—a cruel thing to do, like trying to make two friends into enemies. This kind of talk makes the church the spanking boy every time, implying that it's "spiritual" to refuse to usher, sing in the choir or teach a Sunday School class, so that we can sit home with our families in front of the television with our feet up and munch corn chips.

There is dangerous, twisted thinking here. Let me tell you about my friend Bruce's family of schnauzers. We paid a visit when mama schnauzer had her puppies. The whole family of them were in a playpen in the kitchen. That enclosure was their whole world, and those tiny pups snuggled against their mother for warmth, food, love—everything they needed.

They had no idea that they were totally dependent on a larger family, a human family—Bruce and June and their children—who were (under God) the ultimate source of the provision of all their needs.

Do you have a physical family? Then snuggle close together for warmth, food, and love hopefully provided there. But recognize that your true source of godly love, warmth, nourishment, and togetherness should come from the larger family, the eternal family. Look carefully at the emphasis in the New Testament epistles, God's directions for us in this church age. They tell us to use our gifts to nourish the Body of Christ, and to draw our nourishment from the Body, so that all the adult singles, young people without Christian parents, and marrieds without Christian spouses will feel just as cared for and loved and nourished as anyone else in God's beautiful forever-family. And when we're loved and fed and prayed for there, our lacks and needs in our physical family relationships will be wonderfully met.[1]

Let me suggest another reason why we need the imprint

of the whole family of God upon us. To be shut up to two people, a man and his wife, trying to represent all of God to each other, puts too much pressure on them both. To tell a husband that his words to his wife are the voice of God to her, is going beyond biblical truth, as far as I can see, and also, it is more responsibility on him than he can stand. And then because he doesn't measure up to God, the wife gets terribly frustrated.

More than one wife has come to me at conferences where I've spoken with this typical sad tale: she has a Christian husband who's a good man, but just quiet and not much of a leader. She had always led the children in family devotions until she learned that her husband was supposed to be the "high priest" in the home. (That's straight out of the Old Testament, but even there it would be wrong; there was only one high priest.) So last year some time, she quit leading the family devotions, waiting for her husband to do it. For a year there's been no open Bible reading or prayer in the home; the kids have gotten scattered and rebellious and hard; and she is frantic. What should she do?

I turn to 2 Timothy 1:5. Eunice aggressively transmitted her faith to her son. Probably Grandmother Lois had plenty to say, too. So Timothy's Greek father didn't chip in? So? Whatever we know about Jesus we are responsible to pass on—and certainly that means beginning with our own precious children. I tell this mother to hurry home and open up the Bible again, and pray with her children, and pray that it isn't too late! And I suggest to her to alert any other Christian adults her children happen to like, to help steer them to the Word and prayer as well. And to corral any of their peers who are turned on to Jesus! And to get all the spiritual family to functioning, rather than dropping the whole responsibility in the lap of one man—who may secretly be wringing his hands over feelings of guilt and inadequacy and defeat!

And finally I give her Ephesians 5:33 in the Amplified Version, and tell her to admire and cherish her husband—before him and before others—for all the beautiful things that he is, and not to try to force him to be what he is not.

Another question that constantly comes to me when I speak at conferences is, "If God is to be our first priority, and the Body of Christ is second, and the world is third, where does the family fit in?" Actually, that's trying to fit apples among oranges. The physical family, precious and wonderful as it is, is a social institution. Soon we'd have to set up a list of priorities that also included "masters and slaves," bosses and underlings, governors and citizens, and so on.

But the answer I give them is, "If your family members are Christians, they're the closest, most precious inner circle of 'priority two.' If they're not Christians, they're the closest, most precious inner circle of 'priority three.' " What I'm inferring is that if their family members are not Christians, priority two must still be priority two. From Jesus' own earthly example, we see that our unsaved family's greatest need is to observe a life on fire for God, unswervingly given to Christ and his people and his world. And we must draw all the comfort and motivation and guidance we possibly can from God's family, to show us how to handle those we so long to draw into it!

People ask how we raised our "preachers' kids" who didn't rebel, who grew up loving the church and are spending their lives—the grown ones, at least—ministering to it. I have to say that it's been the grace of God, in spite of many mistakes on our part, that made our children turn out as they have.

But I know the reason our children love the church is that

we love the church! They grew up feeling that where the Body of Christ is, that's where the action is, where the fun is. We took them along as often as possible, because we wanted them exposed to all the important, fun things we were exposed to, and we wanted them exposed to all those wonderful people. Many saints have helped raise our children. They have truly been loving aunts, uncles, and grandparents; they've been extended family. They've given our kids as much security and sense of belonging and being loved as if our children had been raised generations ago on a farm with an extended physical family around them. No—more: the ingredient of the Holy Spirit was added.

Recently our congregation had a time of "lingering before the Lord," as we sometimes do, for four evenings in a row.

One evening during a time of congregational sharing, Lisa came to the front. Lisa is a willowy, beautiful art student, about twenty-two.

"I want to thank the Lord for my mom and dad," said Lisa. "They've raised me to love him, and they've been such wonderful models for me of how to live totally for the Lord. I'm so grateful for them!" And she glanced over at a couple of smiling, teary parents.

"I also want to thank the Lord for other couples who have in a sense helped to raise me—some of my parents' best friends, who have loved me and prayed for me, too." And Lisa named about eight other couples, and she looked around at them. "Thank you; I love you—each of you," said Lisa.

The question parents ask should not be "How much time do I give my family, and how much do I give the church?" How about this instead?—"As for me and my house, we will serve the Lord! Come, wife; come, children; let's go together as often as we can to the church and to Christian homes as in

Acts 2, to give all we can together, and to receive all we can together. We'll draw our physical family into our spiritual family, and hopefully soon they'll be members of both!"

Acts 2:41 says that three thousand new souls were baptized, and the next verse says that they, the three thousand, were "continually devoting themselves" to the new Christian lifestyle, daily in the temple and in homes. I can't believe all three thousand accepted Christ as whole, complete physical family units. They came however they came—by ones, by twos, by threes. But their new lifestyle was so powerful that soon they were joined by five thousand more (Acts 4:4)—surely many from their immediate families. Even the scientific testings of church growth experts in recent years show that conversions spread most easily through families. What our non-Christian physical families most need to see is functioning, authentic Christianity; then they're in a position to be converted, too!

And not just converted. When God's children obey his commandment to "love one another" (1 John 3:23) our physical families are the beneficiaries in every way.

Readers of *Disciplines of the Beautiful Woman* write they've gotten into small groups with the following results:

"My husband is so happy about all the changes (in my life). . . ."

"(Through this) I see the fulfillment of one of my priority goals: 'to see all three kids . . . sold out to God!' *The Keller family for God!* Our children have already done just that. . . ."

"I feel renewed in desire to bring glory to my husband and to help him to be a successful man of God. . . ."

"My husband has even noticed the change, and through me I have seen the Lord work in him. . . ."

All of us who have physical families long for them to be spiritually great for God. The support and prayers of our brothers and sisters in Christ can make this happen. Let's open our eyes to the wonderful family into which God has placed us—and who *need* to minister to us in this way.

And even beyond that: every member of that spiritual family of ours is struggling toward heaven, and has the same longings to be spiritually great for themselves. *They* are also our family members who need help and prayer!

Now, please don't write me a letter asking, "Which do you think I should do on Thursday nights—stay home with my family or go to prayer meeting?" I don't want to give any specific guidance; no two cases would have the same solution, anyway. The Holy Spirit is wonderfully up to showing you what to do on Thursday nights! I'm just seeking to give, as the Lord helps me, a broad principle from the Scriptures.

Several weeks ago Ray and I were ministering to missionaries in Taiwan, and I took down this paragraph from Ray's speaking which states the "broad principle" so well:

> We have belonged to each other since before the foundation of the world. We will belong to each other when the world has no more foundation. When heaven and earth pass away, we will still be God's people. Our relationship together transcends all other relationships.

Inside of every one of the members of your spiritual family lives the Spirit of Christ. How precious they are! Have you looked at them lately with spiritual eyes? Have you remembered how important they are eternally, how precious to God? Are you treating them tenderly? Are you guarding your unity together? Are you disciplining your mind to the mind of Christ and with humility considering one another more important than yourself? (Phil. 2:1–5).

They are co-heirs with you—and along with Christ himself—

of all eternity's vast blessings. They have more wisdom than you or I dream, with the Holy Spirit residing within. Let's respect the older ones as fathers and mothers, and ask their advice. Let's love and encourage the brothers and sisters. Let's feed and cuddle the babies, and be patient and full of hope for their future maturity.

Three cheers for God's fabulous family!

8.

Our New Commandment

It's morning, and I'm still in bed. We're on vacation, and Ray and Nels left very early to go fishing with a friend. Some neighbors are so loud that their voices float through my open window, and I hear a shouted sentence which is crude and vulgar. I recognize the sentence; yesterday I saw it printed on a tee shirt in a shop window. It's great for laughs if morals mean nothing to you.

I turn over, reach for my notebook, and write a thought for this book:

> In these days immorality, like a pack of wolves, is enclosing us on all sides. Unless the sheep bind together tighter than ever, more and more sheep on the fringes of the flock will get snatched. Oh, how close we must move in, or we'll get ripped away, and ripped apart. . . .

That thought may be the most important thought in the book. . . . Lord, cause this book to move around America, Africa, Indonesia, Korea, South America, . . . and may it become a powerful force to bind the sheep together! The wolf packs become bolder and stronger and more open in these days. Put your sheep into units of love that will make them unreachable, untouched! . . .

With that in mind, think about John 13:

A door shuts; a man goes out into the night. Without him there are twelve men left in the room: Jesus and eleven of his disciples around a table. They've taken together the bread and wine of the Last Supper, but there are deep things that could not be said until Judas left. (That's always true. Some special truths God gives only to the faithful when others aren't around.)

And now, in John 13:31—16:33, Jesus gives his deepest and final truths to his eleven before he goes to the cross. And the very first thing he says, as if it were uppermost in his mind and he could hardly wait for Judas to leave to say it, is this:

> "A new commandment I give to you, that you love one another, even as I have loved you, that you also love one another. By this all men will know that you are my disciples, if you have love for one another" (John 13:34–35).

He couches the command in a warning: he says he's going to leave them (v. 33). And here were these eleven men—so diverse in personality and thinking! One had been a semi-traitor, a collaborator with Rome; another was a red-hot Jewish zealot. That was worse than putting together a far-left Democrat with a John Birch Republican! What would be the glue that would hold them together when he left? Love.

"A new commandment I give to you," he says. What was the old commandment, that made this one new? Well, Jesus had spelled it out in Luke 10:27–37: "You shall love the Lord your God with all your heart, and with all your soul, and with all your strength, and with all your mind; and your neighbor as yourself."

"And who is my neighbor?" asked someone. And Jesus told the story of the "Good Samaritan," to show that "my neighbor" is anyone in the world, no matter if his country is different, or his race, or whatever.

"Anyone in the world must love anyone in the world, as much as he loves himself," says the Old Commandment. Wow! That's some kind of high standard, isn't it! Certainly no one has ever come up to God's idea of righteousness.

But the New Commandment is infinitely higher. It's not spoken to just anybody: to eleven men Jesus said, "Love one another." It's a "spiritual family" command, given in the light of the New Testament.

"Love one another"—how? The Old Command was "as you love yourself." The New Command is "as Jesus Christ loves you"! Amazing!

This would completely throw us if we didn't have verses like Romans 5:5: "The love of God has been poured out within our hearts through the Holy Spirit who was given to us."

God never asks anything of us that he doesn't give us the power to do. "The fruit of the Spirit is love" (Gal. 5:22). *He loves in us;* we just need to act it out!

Notice, though, that it *is* a commandment—a tough commandment. It's not just a suggestion or an ideal, given in some ethereal emotion. It's the hardest thing he's asked of us, and the command keeps repeating over and over in the rest of the New Testament. Words like *love, peace,* and *together* occur again and again.

Recently Ray and I were holding a conference together for an evangelical church—a good, happy, healthy one; and at one point we were gathered around a dining table with the pastoral staff.

One of the ministers, a dear guy with a hassled look, said, "I want to tell you honestly that the church scene to me these days is just one blur of potlucks and committee meetings. Frankly, it's a drag. There are plenty of times when I want out."

We answered with sympathy; we have felt that way plenty! But the analogy we used in our answer was marriage: you start off in a romantic pink cloud—but eventually, inevitably, some morning you wake up, look across at that lump in the bed, with its mouth open, and you think, "I'm married to *this*? Yuck!" *At that point* love becomes an act of the will, and of conscious obedience to God. "I am committed to him (or her), and that's that. I *choose* to continue to love, and love with all my being." Later the pink cloud will be there again!

Ordination, we said, was a "pink cloud" experience. Eventually, inevitably, every minister wakes up to the "yuck" feeling! And *at that point,* as for every Christian, loving the Body with all our hearts becomes a conscious act of the will, a commitment-no-matter-what.

But furthermore, we said, the Christians in Acts 2:46 had potlucks, and in Acts 15:4 they had committees—and we have to see these things through spiritual eyes. What are potlucks and committees but opportunities for people to rub off on each other—people who have Jesus Christ inside, in whom is glory, whose destination is heaven? When they interact a mystical thing is happening. And ten years later, after all the potlucks and committees with their ingredients of love and laughter, of pain and patience, of hard times and difficulties and misunderstandings and fighting our way back again to each other—after and through all that, looks of glory begin to grow on our faces!

I'm not just being an idealist. After almost thirty years of being a pastor's wife, almost thirty years of potlucks and committees—yes, the pink cloud is there, as I think, "For better or for worse, these are my people. And I love being committed to them."

Hey—did you ever think—it's just hitting me as I write—surely *committee* and *committed* are from the same root word. I love the thought, anyway.

And one more word from someone I've heard recently (I can't remember who)—that the Christian's sanctification comes from two influences: internally, from the Holy Spirit, and externally, from the Body of Christ. That's good.

Now back to John 13. If Jesus commands us to love each other *as he has loved us,* how does Jesus love us? I see five ways.

First, Jesus loves us with "uttermost" love—a love "to the end," or "to the fullest extent," as we see in John 13:1. That's leaving the pink clouds behind, through all the potlucks and committees—all the way. For Jesus it meant leaving heaven behind, and through all the heat and dust and hassles of Galilee, Samaria, and Judea—all the way up to and including his death and resurrection. Jesus loved us, and loves us, with everything he has, even his very life.

And that's how we're to love each other.

Second, he loves us with a serving love. Look at John 13: 4–5—how he stooped to do slave work as a demonstration of his love.

The refrain of an anthem I've written goes like this:

Think of it, Lord! You gave him seas and sands,
And there he was with a towel in his hands!
Think of it, Lord! You gave him sands and seas,
And there he was, down on his knees! *

---

* "Think of It, Lord," © 1971, 1973 Singspiration, Division of the Zondervan Corporation. All rights reserved.

And that's how we're to love each other. How different from the world, grasping after its rights!

We know a man we always call "Dear Alfred." He has done very well in commercial real estate, but Dear Alfred loves to put on his old clothes and get down on his knees for us, repairing our sprinkler system, painting, fixing a broken hinge—anything. He does it because he loves.

How does Jesus love us? Third, he loves us with a personal, intimate love. He called his disciples to be "with him," as the King James Version says, and his last earthly words were, "Surely I will be with you always" (Matt. 28:20). His love is a love that moves in close. He doesn't stand across the street with a megaphone and call to us, "Now—hear—this! I love you!"

The love of the early Christians was the same: they were daily together in the temple and in homes. There's no substitute for this. Authentic Christian love is intimate love. That's how we're to love each other.

How does Jesus love us? Fourth, with an unconditional love. Jesus loved you; Jesus loves you; Jesus will always love you—period! There is nothing "iffy" about his love. It's not based on performance; it's based on grace. Praise the Lord!

When Romans 15:7 says to us, "Receive one another *as Christ has received you*," we're to love each other with all these facets of love. Whether it's easy or not, that's how we're to love each other.

And fifth, how does he love us? With a responsible love. Christ

> loved the church and gave himself up for her to make her holy, cleansing her by the washing with water through the Word, and to present her to himself as a radiant church, without stain or wrinkle or any other blemish, but holy and blameless (Eph. 5:25–27).

He loves us with a goal in mind: that he will stick with us until we are all that he longs for us to be! That's "tough love."

And that's how we're to love each other.

Friend, we're to be responsible for each others' growth and improvement. We have to care. We have to stick with each other until it happens. In a divided world, believers must demonstrate how God can put people together. You can't be right in your doctrine and wrong in your living!

A team of us were ministering to missionaries in Colombia for ten days in a beautiful time of renewal. At the end of that time one of the missionaries, a good-looking, big ex-Marine, got to his feet and said, "Friends, I've discovered in these days that I'm responsible for you. But I've also discovered that you're responsible for me—and don't you forget it!"

And in all these aspects of love, *love must show*. It must be audible and visible! Why do you think Paul actually had to tell Christians to greet one another with kisses—pure, holy kisses? (Rom. 16:16). Because those people were inhibited just as we are. They were cynical; they were wary; they were shy. And Paul knew that shyness degenerates into coolness—and pretty soon we have a cold church. "Go on," prods Paul, "kiss each other!"

All men will know that we are Jesus' disciples—by the steadfastness of our commitment to each other; by the way we serve each other so selflessly; by our intimacy "with all purity;" by our sacrifices for each other, our words of affirmation and encouragement, our hugs and kisses. . . . By these all men will know . . .

Not by our impressive church buildings—

Not by our charming personalities—

Not by our up-to-date techniques—

By these, says Jesus, "all men will know that you are my very own disciples."

The great sin of Christians today is the sin of withholding love. When people in the world see authentic, biblical love within God's family, they'll believe.

That's scriptural.

That's unexplainable.

That's supernatural.

That's irresistible!

9.

Specific Love

Several years ago Ray and I spent some time in Peru. Lima is the most gorgeous capitol city! It's like old Spain, with South American touches.

Many of the homes have balconies with the upper stories— fabulous, hand-carved wood balconies, where the people can sit and watch the passers-by down on the street below. If they want to, they can converse with them; or in any case, they can converse with each other about what the street people are saying and doing.

I think there are lots of "balcony Christians" in this world. They can see a lot. They know a lot. And they spend their time discussing the "street Christians," the ones who are actually down on the road in the thick of things, accomplishing in the heat and dust of the day.

The "second priority" isn't only to be discussed; it's to be done. We Christians today know so much at a discussion level! But, oh, how we need to *do!* How we need to step out and *obey* new truths as we learn them!

So our first question is something like this: "If I have 496 fellow members at 'First Church' where I'm a member, how can I love them all, deeply and equally?"

In one way you can, if your lifestyle says, "I am committed to all of you, because I share your common way of living; as the early Christians in Acts 2:42-46, I am with you in giving myself to Bible study, fellowship, eating together, and our public worship." Then you plunge in even more deeply by being ready to meet physical needs from your purse.

John Calvin comments on the fact that the King James Version says "all those which believed were *joined together*," and that the Greek says "joined into the same," or "into one," —"which may be expounded of the place, as if he should have said that they were wont to dwell together in one place."

In other words, psychologically, they felt like *family*. And families have a common pot of money! There's certainly ownership in the family (see Acts 5:4). We talk about "John's room" or "Mary's bike." But there's an overall bank account.

People have often laughed at those first Christians about this. Even in Calvin's day they jeered over the early Christians' having "all things in common" and wondered if that included wives. That may be good for a laugh, but the truth of it was a powerful reality.

Even a non-Christian worldling—an entertainer, for instance, or a sports figure—who strikes it rich will take care of his brothers and sisters, or buy his mother a better house. If *he* understands about family, how much more should we, when some of us strike it rich, share with Christian brothers and sisters or parents nearby who are struggling financially? And James 2:15-16 says this proves that our Christianity is authentic.

But beyond this much-needed "life together" in a local Body, there's still an itch that we haven't scratched yet when we hear the question, "I have 496 fellow members at 'First Church.' How can I love them all, deeply and equally?"

I had the same problem when I was a young pastor's wife. Somebody had told me, "Pastors and wives must love everybody equally in the congregation. Don't have any close friends, because that would be playing favorites."

I tried to be a good politician and hug everybody and kiss all the babies—but I had the awful feeling I was missing some. And besides, I would have gotten lonelier and lonelier except, happily, it just didn't work! There were those, God bless them, who moved in to be special friends with *me*, and it was not hard to love them back, with a closeness I couldn't possibly offer to everybody else, much as I wanted to.

Now I know that the policy wasn't *supposed* to work, because it's unbiblical. The Scriptures are full of stories of close friends, and leaders had them, too. Moses had Joshua. Elijah had Elisha. David had his band of thirty men, with three in the inner circle. Jesus had three within twelve, and seventy beyond those. Paul had Barnabas, Silas, Timothy, Luke, Epaphroditus, and many more.

Let me share with you what seems to me to be the ABC's for relational fulfillment in your life.

A: You need accountability to a few other Christians.

Our concept of freedom is apt to be "freedom from everybody," and this freedom is both lonely and ungodly.

Parents, if you want your children to be accountable to you, then you must learn to be accountable to others. Ephesians 5 says that Christians are all to be "subject to one another," and then proceeds with specific relationships: husbands and wives, parents and children, masters and slaves.

Colossians 1:28 says that our goal is to be able to bring each other to maturity in Christ, and 1 Corinthians 12:20–21 says that everybody needs everybody, in order for this to happen! Don't be too independent! We need to say to each other in

God's family, "Hold me to my commitment! Don't let me go! I need you!"

B: You need brokenness. Proud, stiff people don't bend. God thought it was terrible for the Israelites to be stiffnecked! Brokenness is precious to him.

David held out for a whole year after his "big sin" before writing Psalm 51, when he confessed that "the sacrifices of God are a broken spirit; a broken and contrite heart, O God, thou wilt not despise" (Ps. 51:17). Up until that fresh brokenness, it must have been a terrible year (Ps. 32:1–4).

When you're not broken—when you're stiff, proud, and afraid—you'll never be accountable to others, and you'll never get any help for yourself. Go to the cross, and ask the Lord Jesus to open you up and make you a real person! There is no person so alone as the person who is alone with his sin.

But don't try to break each other. Being broken and exposed is strictly a voluntary thing.

C: You need cleansing. Hosea 14:2 says, *"Take words with you,* and return to the Lord. *Say to him,* 'Forgive all our sins. . . .' "

For so many years we've said to our children, "Say you're sorry!" Being sorry without saying so isn't very sorry! And in the family of God, learning to say "I'm sorry," and to stay cleansed in all our relationships with each other, is absolutely essential.

Take a check on yourself. You need a longing for accountability; you need a broken spirit; and you need fresh (and continual) cleansing. Then you're ready to proceed with the nitty-gritty "how-to's" of relationships in the family of God. Are you ready?

Dr. Peter Wagner, church growth expert and our friend "Pete" to us as a dear member of our church, analyzes the success of Lake Avenue Congregational Church as coming because we expose our people to three levels of commitment, each of which Pete begins with the letter C: [1]

The "celebration" is the big Sunday time when everybody joins together to worship God. It doesn't matter how many are there; we could have thousands more, and it would be just as fulfilling. We are there to be one-on-one with God, to fellowship with him and enjoy him.

The "congregation" must not be more than 200. Our "congregations" are our Sunday school classes. Around 1200 adults are in classes each Sunday at Lake Avenue, in addition to our children. Here we not only learn the Bible but we relate to our peers. Most classes are according to age, with 40 to 175 in a class, and within them we socialize, exchange casseroles when we're sick, and have a general feeling of belonging. Pete says that people can relate socially to only about 120 people, so, lately, when several of our classes have gotten consistently over the upper limit, we've split them, and they've kept on growing.

For many churches the "congregation" and the "celebration" are one and the same, but when church attendance gets up to 200, there needs to be some kind of smaller groupings so the people don't lose their sense of sociability and belonging.

Mostly out of our Sunday school classes come our home small groups, which Pete calls the "cell." We say they function best with between four and eight people; so all Lake Avenue members who are willing are exposed, weekly at least, to the "celebration" of several thousand, to their own "congregation" of 40–175, and to their "cell" of four to eight. The small group is not to be another Bible class, for more information; it's the place where people can get healed and helped on an individual basis, as they share their lives in an atmosphere of love and acceptance.

People tell us they're surprised to find a *big* church such a warm church. We don't see why we couldn't grow to any number of thousands and not lose our warmth, as long as we help our people to stay involved in all three of these levels of commitment and love.

So what do *you* as an individual need to do? First, you need to make sure that you're in the family of God at all. Have you been "born again"? Have you come to God at some point in your life, seeing your sin and need, and accepting the forgiveness he offers through the gift of salvation by his Son, the Lord Jesus Christ?

That minimal step, so simple but so all-important, places you in the Body of Christ, in the family of God, an eternal, spiritual group whose exact numbers are known only to God.

Then you need to do several outward things, as visible signs of the inward change (Acts 2:42). You need to find the right church, be baptized publicly before its members, and put your name on its membership roll. It's not the true invisible church, but it's the visible one, comparable to the "church at Philippi" or the "church at Thessalonica," through which the Holy Spirit does his working during this church age.

How do you find the right one? No visible church is going to be perfect, and the Lord's plan is probably for you to see some faults and join it anyway—just as they may see faults in you and accept you anyway! That's how God brings maturity to us all. Nevertheless, there are some basics. They need to hold to Christ as the eternal Son of God, the Savior from our sins through his death, the true head of the church. 1 John 4:1–3 says to be careful not to fall for doctrinal error.

What will help a church stay doctrinally correct is loving, teaching, and preaching the Bible, so look for that. When the preaching is all philosophy and psychology, and the Sunday school classes are discussions of what everybody thinks, look out! "There is a way that seems right to a man, but in the end it leads to death" (Prov. 16:25). The Bible needs to be in their hands, to be used and marked and loved.

But beyond *truth* there needs to be *grace*. Jesus was full of both (John 1:14). A church can hold to wonderful truth but be totally dead, and not even know it—or be totally belligerent in the way they hold to the truth! Is there a real sense of worshiping the Lord in the church services? Do they love to mention his name in their conversations? Are there new Christians among them, and new ones being born again? Look for signs of life!

If the Lord seems to lead you to feel you've found your spiritual home, join them. Be baptized if you haven't done that yet, and get your name on the membership list. Yes, that's important! Don't have your membership back in good old Smithville, just because your ancestors are buried there. Take your stand with the local Body, which says, "I'm one of you. I belong to you. I want to submit to you and share your life in Christ."

Then immerse yourself as deeply as you can into the life of that local Body. Worship right among them—not by radio or television at home; not even sitting out in the narthex. "But I can hear it over the speaker" isn't good enough. You need to be shoulder to shoulder, sharing the others' reactions to it all, and letting them share yours. They need to hear you sing! They need to catch the intensity of your worship.[2]

You'll be caught up, then, in the celebration. Great! But you also need some sort of "congregation" of a few dozen who can get to know who you are. They know your name; you know theirs. You see each other at parties, Bible classes, church doings. They help you know you belong, and you help them know they belong!

And beyond that, you need at least one "cell" in your life. That's so important, let's take a new chapter for it.

10.

Your Own Small Group

Out of dozens or hundreds, you need a few. Even if your church is small, you need a special few. When our daughter Margie and her husband John went to pastor their very first church there were only a handful; but John got them into small groups, and love made them grow and grow!

And if your Sunday congregation is large, how can you really share your life with everyone? Or if your Sunday school class or Bible class is large, how can you deeply love them all? You can't. You shouldn't. You can enjoy them and have fun with them and feel a part of them. But for the struggles in your life and the dreams and goals you have; for the correction you need—yes, and the correction you need to give; for all your nitty-gritty daily affairs to be supported and prayed for and guided, you need a group of four to eight.

How can you find them? Maybe you're already in a Christian "grouping" of that size, and you just need to begin to function! When Lake Avenue Church began to realize the implications of the "three priorities," it was the board of trustees first, if I remember correctly, who woke up to the fact that they needed to function according to the priorities to which they said they were committed. The head of the board at that time said, "Hey, fellows, if these three priorities are working in our lives, we can't just have a brief devotional and read the minutes of the former meeting and do business. We have to act out our commitments together!"

So first they gave themselves to the worship of God. They spent time in singing or prayer or whatever would focus directly on him, and they took adequate time to tell him they loved him.

Then they spent time on the second priority. They shared where they were in their lives since their last meeting, and they prayed for each other. If these things took an hour or more, so be it. Meeting around Christ and then caring for each other were the most important parts of their business. And it's interesting that Ray says if a fellow was late and missed those first parts, you could tell it. He was more apt to be argumentative and uptight when they got to the trustee business.

But because of that breakthrough the trustees became more than a board; they became a loving unit, a functioning part of a living organism. And since then, all our boards and committees in the church seek to operate the same way.

Also at that time, on Monday mornings there were half a dozen women in the vault of a local bank counting the previous day's offerings. They became a "small group," and added breakfast to extend the fellowship, and through the years have become exceedingly dear to each other.

I remember a meeting of our church women's executive board when one of the women, a "mother figure" to the rest, who were considerably younger, became truly broken—perhaps for the first time. It was well into the year's meetings, and we'd gotten comfortable with each other, and she told us, "All through the years I was thought of as a spiritual person because my husband was. Actually, he was the only one of us memorizing Scripture and studying and witnessing and having time for a deep prayer life. And since he died, I'm discovering that I don't have his coattails to ride on any more, and I'm feeling very empty. Please pray for me, that I'll become a godly person in my own right!"

Believe me, we didn't despise her for that; we admired her and loved her more than ever. And we felt close enough to her, for the first time, to know where she was and what her goals were and how to pray for her. Needless to say, God has answered our prayers, and she is living a wonderfully productive life!

If you're in another kind of Christian grouping but it's too large, maybe you can extend your time and split in half or more, to become "small groups" for part of your time together.

Or maybe you're in nothing like that at all. How do you find some others and get started? Ask the Lord! This is all his business, and he's very eager to help us with it. Maybe after you've prayed, you'll feel drawn to take the initiative and ask certain ones. Maybe after you've prayed, others will ask you. The point is prayer—and God loves to answer prayer. Furthermore, he's the great administrator of the church and knows just how to organize it for the greatest spiritual effectiveness!

Notice in Luke 6:12 and following how Jesus narrowed down from many to twelve. When we give ourselves to a "small group," it seems to me we are following Christ's method, and Paul's method, and so on. In Luke 6:12 you see that Christ also prayed before he picked and started his "small group." Prayer didn't ensure that everybody in the group was going to be perfect and ideal; Judas was one of the twelve! All the members of our groups may not turn out to be saintly saints;

but if the group has been formed out of prayer, they will still be right.

Now, when Jesus had picked the Twelve out of all his disciples, Luke 6 describes physically the way Jesus' lifestyle was going to look relationally, from here on. Look at verses 17 and 18:

> He went down [from the mountain] with [the Twelve] and stood on a level place. A large crowd of his disciples was there and a great number of [other] people . . . who had come to hear him and to be healed of their diseases. . . .

If you looked at this scene from a helicopter, you'd see Jesus in the middle, ringed with concentric circles. Closest around him were the Twelve. In a ring around them were the multitude of his other disciples; and outside of that ring were all the rest of the curiosity seekers and "believers" of one degree or another.

Notice verses 19 and 20: "And the people all tried to touch him. . . . And looking at his disciples, he said. . . ."

Do you see the great difference in the relationships? The crowds were satisfied to touch. And there certainly was healing and help in the touch of Jesus. Praise the Lord for all the multitudes in the world today who believe in him and who've been touched by him in some way!

But the word *disciple* means "learner." What a difference! Jesus touched the crowds, but he taught the disciples. He deliberately turned to them and gave them his time, attention, teaching, and close-in love.

Notice how special their place was, in Luke 7:11: "Soon afterward, Jesus went to a town called Nain; and his disciples and a large crowd were going along with him."

You get the feeling of concentric circles again. And as the days moved along, the crowds came and went, and even, probably, the disciples came and went; but soon Luke is more specific: "After this, Jesus traveled about from one town and village to another.... The Twelve were with him" (Luke 8:1).

And Luke 8:4 says that when a large crowd gathered, he taught them by parable; but verse 9 says that privately to the Twelve he explained what the parable meant.

Luke 9:1 says that soon he gave special power and authority to the Twelve, and both Luke 8:51 and 9:28 show that by now he was singling out three of the Twelve for the deepest times of all with him.

We know Jesus' message very well; we can recite John 3:16 at the drop of a hat. But we are just beginning to realize his method—and oh, how we need it! Jesus did many wonderful things for the multitudes, but more and more, as his three years went along, he invested his time in a few. We need to catch that, and act on it.

What qualities did the Twelve have that made Jesus choose them? What qualities should you look for, when you pray over whom you should get close to? I see at least three qualities.

One: these people were *available*. For instance, there was Levi, or Matthew as he was called. How about this?—"After this, Jesus went out and saw a tax collector by the name of Levi sitting at his tax booth. 'Follow me,' Jesus said to him, and Levi got up, left everything and followed him" (Luke 5:27–28).

This doesn't mean that Levi never had any earthly possessions from this point on. When he "left everything," it simply meant that he had a new master who would take charge of everything Levi owned. The very next verse says that Levi's first act as a follower of Jesus was to use his own house to throw a big party and introduce all his friends to Jesus—all the other tax-gatherers and the whole bunch! (Luke 5:29). What a thrill!

There are many Christians who are not really available for small groups. They have great personalities, and you'll always enjoy them and feel warm toward them—but maybe they're not loose enough from this world system really to commit themselves to you at close range. Anyway, not for now. Don't break your heart over them.

Second: I see that Jesus' disciples were *teachable*. That's what makes a disciple; we know already that the word means "learner," and he's willing to be one. He can't give the impression of already knowing everything! Jesus' disciples said, "Teach us to pray" (Luke 11:1). Some Christians are always teaching you; their communication just goes in one direction. That doesn't make for give-and-take in a sharing situation.

Third: Jesus' disciples had *heart!* You have to look for heart in people! That is, when you mention the Lord, you see a little sparkle in their eye. Something lights up; you have the feeling you could communicate around the Lord together. Neither one of you has to know a lot, but God gives you the feeling that it would go. "Heart" means everything. More than sharpness or education, although it's good to have things in common, look for a longing to know God better!

Actually, when you get together with a small group of other believers, you're discipling. If that scares you, remember they're also discipling you. But Jesus' last words to his Twelve were, "Now I'm leaving you, so you turn around and disciple others, just as I've discipled you. See that they're baptized, and teach them everything you've learned from me" (Matt. 28: 18–20). And that's what the Twelve went out and did, and the result is that we have the church today.

He didn't even say, "Go out and evangelize"; he said, "Go make disciples." Not all of us are evangelists; that's a special gift; but all Christians must be disciplers. He didn't say "Go have occasional crash programs." These often wear out the saints, and the results can be almost nil.

No, little by little, line upon line and precept upon precept, Christians are to disciple each other; we're to act on each other. And then, more particularly, the more mature are to disciple the less mature; and the ones who know little are to learn from those who know more; and in this way the whole family of God acts out its roles and grows in him (2 Tim. 2:2).

New believers start out as the children at first. They learn from many fathers and mothers, at close range, with time enough to let the learning relate to their daily lives and get it all worked in, in application. Eventually (hopefully soon!) they'll be parenting others.

This isn't easy. It's why the ABC's are all important. They may be the "big shots" in business, or have years of maturity and knowledge in many areas. To humble themselves enough to be accountable to others, and to be broken in spirit, will not be easy.

You think about Paul. Sometimes we think of him as a very young man when he met Christ. Actually, scholars tell us he was probably in his forties. He was a respected Pharisee and more: a member of the exclusive Sanhedrin, like our Supreme Court. In his career and in his personality, Paul was in cement. He was hardened into his loves and hates.

Suddenly he meets Jesus! By instant blindness he is made physically dependent on others. For three days he's led by the hand like a little child. Then he's delivered into the hands of a "big brother" in God's family, Ananias, to whom he's to submit for counseling and instruction. Paul is a brand-new little brother in Christ!

Or take Nicodemus, another religious "heavy." He'd been an authority for probably a long time, to whom others went for instruction. When he came to Jesus, he made himself vulnerable. He came humbly, as a learner; he asked for it, and he got it! Maybe John 3:10–12 was the first time he'd been rebuked since he was a very young man.

The Interpreter's Bible, commenting on this passage, says there's no credit in being a "bovine" (cowlike) creature who just doesn't understand what he's getting into; but the man of true courage will gather up his fears, his awkwardness at the unfamiliar, and come to Jesus, anyway!

That's how people are "born again" into God's family. Grown men, able women, important people recognized for their skills and status, have to have the courage to step over into God's family and play a brand-new role: they're a new "little spiritual brother or sister" with much to learn.

Remember that Jesus called over a little child, set him in the midst, and said, "I tell you the truth, unless you change and become like little children, you will never enter the kingdom of heaven. Therefore, whoever humbles himself like this little child is the greatest in the kingdom of heaven" (Matt. 18:3–4).

So first we see that a person mature in the family of this world has to be willing to be born again and open up his mind and heart and eyes and ears to a new world. And he has to play a brand new role, that of "baby brother," and be willing to go to the places where he can learn, and where he can ask foolish questions. He has to be willing to submit to teaching and to being loved and cared for and advised, if he's to grow.

Secondly, the parents and big brothers and sisters in God's family must be willing to assume their roles. They must give him plenty of time, feeding information, tenderly rebuking, pointing out Scriptures, and simply reacting to life in front of him so that he can learn how Christians react to life. . . . They must do and be everything that's needed to bring that spiritual baby, through the power of the Holy Spirit, to maturity.

But if Christians don't see the functions of the members of the family of God, they won't see each other with spiritual eyes. They won't see a newly converted "big shot" as a new baby brother. They'll simply see him as a "big shot," and he'll be encouraged to talk too much and not listen enough. Then he'll be cheated and his growth stunted.

In God's family we play completely different roles from those the world knows. And it's essential that we understand them and that we function, in order to help each other grow strong in Christ.

Dick is our neighbor across the street. He's tall and handsome, with a winning personality; he's been very successful in business and is known around Pasadena as a "big man around town." Three years ago last Easter Dick and his wife visited Lake Avenue Church for the first time, and Dick raised his hand in response to Ray's invitation to accept Christ as Savior.

Right away Dick got involved in all three "levels of commitment." He came faithfully to worship services. He joined one of the adult Sunday school classes, and soon was given the job of introducing first-time visitors every week. As soon as he was invited into a small group of men meeting weekly in our living room, Dick accepted. Betty, his wife, who received the Lord soon after Dick, did the same; she got into a small group of women, and the two of them joined a weekly couples' group as well.

Tall Dick is a beautiful "Exhibit A" of a "star" in this world humbly assuming the "little brother" role. He has eagerly exposed himself for three years to everything that's come along that would help him grow—and grow he has. His testimony before groups is so doctrinally clear, and so fervent and convincing, that he is already very important in God's family.

Roles change within the family, as they change in the physical family. I watch Nels these days; our man-child is becoming less son and more brother to us every day. At not quite fourteen he's taller than I am; his voice has dropped; and he's suddenly gotten to taking my arm, telling me what to do, and acting protective of me. I almost feel like saying, "Hey, young punk, I'm 54, not 95." But I don't, because I kind of like it.

Incidentally, Nels is getting so big, I'm sure this is my very last time to tell in a book something funny he's said. I feel very nostalgic about this! Well, here it is.

Recently I sent him into a drugstore to buy a thermometer. Nels doesn't know much about thermometers, and besides, apparently he can sometimes read carelessly.

"Sure, Mom," said Nels. "What kind shall I get—oval or rectangle?"

Well, what I really meant to say is, every so often either Ray or I make a certain speech to Nels. With variations, it goes something like this:

> Jesus was twelve when he gave evidence of being more aware of his heavenly Father than his physical father. We look for that to happen more and more to you, Nels. Through your teens we expect to have to tell you less and less, as you get more and more direction from the Lord. Don't think we'll always be telling you what to do! We pretty much directed your steps the first

twelve years or so, but the more we see you following your heavenly Father, the more we'll back off from now on.

And when you're grown, you'll just be our brother in Christ and our friend, as Sherry and Margie and Bud are now. We'll just enjoy you! But you'll always be God's son and answerable to him, just as we are answerable to him.

But before I close this chapter, let me tell you one more wonderful "baby brother" story. A while back, one of my friends at church drew me aside and said, "Anne, can you come out to the curb? There's someone sitting in a car I want you to meet." Out I went, and here in a car sat this beautiful old man. My friend said, "He's 102 years old, and I led him to the Lord this week."

102! His skin was so pink behind his horn-rimmed glasses that I didn't think he looked more than 75, but when he spoke, he sounded like 150! In a quaver that often cracked into a whisper, this old, old man spoke humble, sweet, baby-brother words. He said, "I was thinking about heaven the other day, realizing that I really wasn't ready to go there, when God sent this wonderful young man along to point me the way!"

It's never too late to be born again! Hallelujah! A person is never too old to become a spiritual baby—if he's willing!

And the world is full these days of new babies in the family of God. But so few of the other members of the family have realized—and assumed—their roles!

Are you an aunt, a father, a grandmother in God's family?

There's a little girl, a little boy, down the street from you or around the corner who has just received Jesus as Savior. Maybe it happened in a Child Evangelism class or at Sunday school, and this little one's parents are not yet Christians.

Or maybe there's an adult you know, who likes you, who's just begun to believe in Jesus Christ as Savior.

What are you going to do about it?

11.

"How To's" for Your Small Group

Last fall a big hole was dug in a vacant lot in Pasadena. We've wondered about that vacant lot for years, because there it was, in the middle of a prime residential area. Pasadena is surrounded by Los Angeles and the ocean on the west, by mountains on the north, and by other towns on the east and south. We can't grow out, we can only grow up, and every foot of ground is precious, so vacant lots are rare.

Finally a hole was dug in this remaining piece. Ray and Nels and I speculated on what the house would be like. "I hope they don't put in a little ranch type; it wouldn't fit the area," I said. "It's going to be great," said Nels.

The winter rains delayed the building, but at last we could see that it was going to be two stories. "Maybe it will be too futuristic and modern," I worried. Ray said, "It ought to be traditional." "It's going to be great," said Nels.

Eventually we could see it was a true luxury home—traditional with arches and second-story balconies and a spectacular rear porch that we could see from the side street. "Now they ought to paint it a quiet earth color," I said. "It's going to be *great*," said Nels.

We parked the car at last and walked around the house. It's putty color, with white trim. The rear patio leads down to a beautiful Jacuzzi. The pool is surrounded by used brick. Inside, the stairway winds gracefully within the two-story-high front hall.

"I told you it would be great," said Nels.

It's great.

What we've been building in this book is a study of the relationships and roles of God's people, his spiritual family. So far we've dug the hole and laid the foundation: we've laid out the biblical basis underneath the relationships and roles.

Now it's time to put up the superstructure, and that's the visible part, the fun part! This is how it's to work out in your life.

Our dear, wise, big son Bud has given me some advice at this point. "Don't let the readers think, Mother, that if they do this, this, and this—that those deeds will make them godly."

Oh, that's absolutely right! Only God can make us godly! It's not our deeds that can transform us into Christlike people, but the deeds of Christ himself, living his life through us.

That's why you needn't be frustrated over the New Commandment, wondering if you can ever love other Christians as Christ loves you. You can't, in your own power. But Christ will love his love in you and through you to other believers, as you let him! Whatever his Word says to you through the principles in this book, his Spirit within you is all the power you'll ever need to carry it out. Do you think you'll ever realize in your life the kind of loving lifestyle you dream of? Let Romans 5:5 answer that for you: "God has poured out his love into our hearts by the Holy Spirit, whom he has given us."

Be encouraged as you get to the "application" part of this book!

I feel comfortable with the format that first states doctrine, then application. Did you ever notice that the first half of Galatians (three chapters) is doctrinal and the last half (three chapters) is application? That the first half of Ephesians (three chapters) is doctrinal and the last half (three chapters) is application? That the first half of Philippians (two chapters) is doctrinal and the last half (two chapters) is application? That the first half of Colossians (two chapters) is doctrinal and the last half (two chapters) is application?

Each first half says, "Here are the doctrinal facts." And each last half says, "Now, here's how you live them out practically."

The first half of this book has given you some doctrinal facts in laying the foundation—the biblical basis for those precious, wonderful relationships between believers. Now up goes the superstructure, where you can see it and put it to work in your life, and others can see it, too, and be affected by it.

We've already talked about your need to be born again into God's family and be baptized and join the local church that's right for you. We've talked about the fact that within the church you have a need for three levels of commitment.

You need to be committed to the "celebration," where you worship God and are fed his Word at least weekly with everyone else in the church.

Second, you need to be committed to a "congregation," a group of from 25 to 200 people—all or part of that church—with whom you relate socially, feel you belong, have fun, and maybe even get "fed" some more.

And third, you need to be committed to a "cell," a small group of from four to eight people. Let's zero in on the cell, and get some help on how to begin really to function in God's family.

Right away I want to say that my suggestions for conducting

a small group are not *the* way; they are only *a* way. They may be too American for your culture, or too big-city—or in many ways not suitable for your situation. Just adapt whatever his Spirit suggests, and he will tailor-make your lifestyle in obedience to him.

What we do see from God's Word is that he wants believers to relate to each other in closeness, reality, and love. Small groups are a way for you to begin to do that. If you have *no* way—here, at least, is *a* way!

The cell isn't really a once-a-week meeting; it's a relationship. It's just like in the physical family, where you're *always* a son or mother or whatever, but hopefully you sit down together every evening for dinner, or every morning for breakfast. So the "small group" of spiritual family members feel they belong to each other and are always on call day or night—but, say, once a week or perhaps oftener, they have a rendezvous. That appointment is not to be broken unless for a very special reason!

I meet Thursday mornings for a two-hour brunch with seven other gals. They're all housewives from 28 to 40, and what a beautiful, eager bunch! I love them so much.

One of them, Jan, is a substitute school teacher, but she assured me when she joined us that she'd never accept Thursday jobs. Soon after we started meeting, a principal approached her with a very special offer of a full-time teaching assignment in just the kind of situation Jan loves.

"I can't do it," she told him. "I'm committed to a Bible study and prayer group on Thursday mornings. Otherwise, I would have loved it."

"I really want you, Jan," he said.

"I truly am sorry," she answered.

And the next thing she knew, she had the job; he'd arranged

for a permanent substitute for her every Thursday morning. And she also had a special new Christian standing in the eyes of that principal!

Besides that, when one student turned out to be really difficult to handle, Jan had seven sisters praying for her daily, and she had a wonderful undergirding of strength in what she had to do.

Why Four to Eight?

Why have we learned that from four to eight seems a good size? Occasionally Christians may meet one on one, but actually it seems richer and better use of time to relate to at least four. It's good to be stretched to love at least four people deeply at one time, and that many interpersonal relationships will help you grow.

But more than eight? Then some members begin to get anonymous. A Bible teaching situation, which is informational, can have a thousand members. But the sharing of lives takes time, so if the groups grow, they need to split—and multiply by dividing!

How Often?

How often should you meet together? Most of our groups do so once a week, but not all. I know of a group of couples and singles in their twenties who meet formally every other week. They feel it's enough because they're already neighbors who see each other many times a week, and they're in close touch for prayer and communication.

More often the variation leans to several times a week. Another one-evening-a-week couples' group I know often has a picnic or home potluck Sunday noons after church, so that their kids can get involved in each others' lives. And I've known business men and young people who made a pact to pray with each other daily over the telephone.

Who?

Who should be in a group together, anyway? I think the only hard-and-fast rule here is not to make hard-and-fast rules! What does *not* work is to administrate it heavily from above, herding people into groups, picking and training leaders and telling them what to do, and so on. Never post names on a bulletin board!—dividing people by neighborhoods or by alphabet or in any other artificial way. Ray and I have found, from lots of years of experience and observation, that we're just to teach the *need* for small groups, and the biblical *reasons* for them, and then let the Holy Spirit take it from there. The people simply find each other; it stays a "grass roots" movement, dictated only by the people's wishes, needs, and sense of obedience.

And besides, God has made his people so innovative that when left to his Spirit's promptings, they think of lots more creative ways to love each other and help each other grow than if one "brain" or committee of brains from above is responsible. Hang loose, brothers and sisters!

Do You Mix the Sexes?

But who should be in a group together? The Bible seems to infer that if it's to be truly a discipling situation, you shouldn't mix the sexes. You've seen the stickiness that comes when a girl seeks to win a fellow to the Lord: tinges of romance are likely to creep in and cloud the issues. Or if a guy tries to teach and disciple a girl—he thinks she's studying the difference between faith and works, and she's thinking how pretty his brown eyes are.

So Jesus discipled men, and Paul discipled Timothy and other men, and Titus 2:3–5 says that mature women are to disciple younger women. It just makes more sense that way.

We've found it also gives a certain freedom to go deeper. When a man wants to ask another godly man how to be a better husband to his wife, he's going to feel a little inhibited, asking, if she's right there in front of him.

But another thing we've found is that, within the sexes, it's beautiful to mix singles and marrieds. Why shouldn't single women, for instance, learn the struggles and joys that wives have? Why shouldn't wives learn about the problems and special lifestyle of singles? Often they're so segregated from each other that they don't learn to appreciate the others' situations. And small groups are the perfect way to mesh singles into physical families, exposing them to their "spiritual kids"!

Two Kinds of Groups

I've been talking about actual discipling, in which the spiritually younger seek out the older and say, "Please teach us and let your lifestyle rub off on us. We want to learn from you." There the sexes probably shouldn't mingle.

But often small groups are actually just "supportive fellowships," where more-or-less peers get together and say, "You teach me what you know about Jesus, and I'll teach you what I know. And where you're strong and I'm weak, you help me; and where I'm strong and you're weak, I'll help you, so we can grow together."

Supportive fellowships can be just one sex, or they can be couples, or they can be couples and singles mixed together. Or why shouldn't they be parents and teenage children mixed together—their own physical children, or others willing to adopt spiritual moms and dads for a while?

Mixing couples and singles is a wonderful way for widows to have some *men* in their lives. I would think one of the real blows for a woman in losing her husband is to discover that she's suddenly shunted to a women's world, and she's expected to spend her time just with the other widows. Terrible! She needs men in her life as she's always had men in her life, to be a whole, balanced person. In a small group she can enjoy being a sister and having brothers. When God's family is truly functioning, the holes and scars and weaknesses and broken parts of the physical-family situation are filled in and healed and mended and completed. Then we live full, balanced lives, with all the richness of relationships that we need!

Right now names may be popping into your head. Are there those you think of that you'd really love to get together with and share the Lord? Get away in a time of concentrated prayer. If he seems to indicate that this group is right, either they'll ask you, or you'll ask them. It will happen, and it will be wonderful!

Should Small Groups Be Forever?

Profit from our experience in something, though; we had to learn the hard way! It never occurred to Ray and me when we were new at this to suggest cut-off times. And so the groups went on and on! Some of them are still going, and many others have petered out.

Without cut-off times, you've got two real dangers: cliques

or failures. Especially in small churches you have to avoid cliques!

When Margie and John, our second daughter and her pastor husband, went to their first little church in rural California, John began his ministry by announcing that Margie would meet with any women who wanted to come on Tuesday mornings, and John would welcome any men on Friday nights for some volleyball and fellowship. Over the months the women's group outgrew their living room and split into Tuesday and Thursday groups. Then they split again and went to other homes. The men's group divided and multiplied, too, and in less than five years John and Margie had a strong, healthy congregation who knew how to care for each other.

Every group needs periodic freshening, so if the original core is committed to stay together, new ones need to be taken in from time to time. Especially look for new Christian babies, who must get loved at close range and assimilated into intimate fellowship if they're going to grow!

But otherwise, the healthy way to start a group is to say, "Let's meet for six months." "Let's meet for this school year." "Let's meet until a certain date." My Thursday morning group is from Easter to Thanksgiving, with a break during the summer.

When your closing date is reached, if you all have a strong conviction that God isn't through with you *together* yet, you may vote to extend for three months or so. But better to quit when you're all loving it than to wait until you don't!

And the thing is, there are so many around you needing, and maybe wanting, a small group! If you close your doors to them, they're on the outside looking in. How important it is for a pastor and his wife to have small groups just over certain periods, so that others know that their turn may be next!

And in a large church, it's an essential way to get to know

intimately your future leadership. Almost all our church officers have been previously in small groups with Ray. They know and understand him, and he knows and understands them. And he has trained them as well as loved them, so that even a large church can be "all of a piece" and operating under the same philosophy of ministry—the three priorities—together.

I must add that occasionally, but rarely, relationships within a small group refuse to "cut off," and they become a lifetime, Jonathan-and-David thing.

Carl and Dewey were in a group together years ago, and not only met weekly but prayed together regularly through the week over the telephone. Their wives also grew to be good friends.

Eventually there came a time when the city of Pasadena needed a new Christian bookstore, and Ray threw out the challenge to our congregation, encouraging someone to start one that would be an outreach of our church but financially independent of it.

Carl and Dewey felt each other out. Carl was a dentist; Dewey managed a hamburger drive-in stand.

"Dewey," said Carl, "I'll give my money if you'll give your time."

So Dewey quit his hamburgers and rushed off to the annual Christian Booksellers' Convention which was just about to convene. Carl committed his life savings, and by fall they'd rented a building almost across the street from the church; they'd remodeled and painted, and their wives had decorated it, and "Christian Corner" was in business.

From the start it was a sensational store. Write-ups buzzed about it from coast to coast; and barely two years later, Word

Music Publishers gave it their national award as "music dealer of the year," with a trip to Hawaii for Dewey and his wife.

"Christian Corner" is four years old this month. I stopped writing for a minute just now to phone Dewey for permission to tell this story, and he said to me, "Anne, people warned us that 'no ship sinks like a partnership.' But Carl and I walked into this because of our hearts' commitment in the Lord to each other. We knew that's how we would handle tough money problems and business situations and deciding who was boss and all the rest of it. Our commitment as brothers in Jesus is the foundation of the whole business."

Well, that's a Jonathan-David relationship for you. which has ended in great glory to God, and which began in a small group.

Small Group Leadership

Does a group have to have a special leader? Well, obviously, if Christians have asked an older Christian to disciple them, the leader is already built-in. But in a supportive fellowship, you can pick your own, or take turns, or whatever you want to do. There does need to be some kind of low-key guidance, at least; a leader keeps a group on schedule and thinks through variety and freshness.

Our Thursday evening group are just peers meeting together. The couples are all in our church, but Ray and I don't consider ourselves the leaders. We probably need them far more than they need us, and they're probably smarter, too. For a while, whosever living room we met in, that husband would lead. But then we liked Lee's leadership so much, we asked him to do it all the time for a while.

If some think of themselves only as followers, beautiful! Just the ones who want to, can take turns leading. Nothing has to be forced.

Group Membership from the Same Church?

One other question often asked me when I'm speaking at conferences: should the members of a small group always be from the same church? Not necessarily; God may bring his children together in different ways. Four of us neighbors meet together, and the four are from three churches.

But I certainly see the value of being from the same church, where the input has been more the same. When you can comment on the pastor's sermons together, and simply be moving along in your Christian lives under many of the same stimuli, you certainly feel the increased closeness in growing together. To say nothing of what it does in binding together a local congregation!

12.

What You Do When You're Together

Recently I heard Dr. Sherwood Wirt preach; he's the editor-emeritus of Billy Graham's *Decision* magazine. There I sat, with my Bible and trusty brown notebook, and what do you suppose Dr. Wirt spoke on? The need of Christians to love one another! And here's a direct quote:

> The New Testament was not written primarily to raise the moral tone of the church; it was not written primarily to promote evangelism over the world. The New Testament was written primarily to get Christians into a loving relationship with each other.

Amen, and I second the motion! And then he quoted Romans 5:5, about how "the love of God has been poured out within our hearts through the Holy Spirit who was given to us"; and he said that "to be filled with the Holy Spirit is to be filled with love."

This is exciting to me, because what Dr. Wirt was preaching about, and what I am writing about, is the crux of the gospel for Christians. "This is my new commandment to you," said Jesus, "that you love one another."

There you are. And love is not just some warm feeling. Love has to be audible, visible, and measurable; it has to be acted out in specific words and deeds that take time, planning, and inconvenience. If you're filled with the Holy Spirit, his fruit will be love in your life. And your calendar will show it, and your conversations and enthusiasms and heart's interests will prove it. And God will be obeyed and glorified!

So what do you do, practically, when you're together? First off, when you've decided on how long you'll meet together and what day of the week and what time, hold faithfully to that time slot. It's important to be prompt, because that's an expression of Christian love! Your arriving on time says, "I consider *your* time more valuable than *my* time, so I didn't want to keep you waiting."

Then it's important to end on time, because otherwise, busy people will be afraid of being trapped. And just as one advantage in a cut-off time is that it makes each session that much more precious, so one advantage to ending on the dot is that it makes each *moment* you're together that much more precious! You don't dawdle! And you don't gossip. You've met around Christ, and you have an agendum. He is in the midst, and you're handling affairs of eternity.

Our Thursday morning group meets supposedly at 9:45, but everyone comes around 9:30 to start on their first cup of coffee and catch up on each others' lives in chatter, so that we can begin right on time. To me, those are acts of love without a word! It's not that they're not busy and can't think of anything else to do; their coming early speaks volumes of their eagerness to be together.

I see at least five ingredients to a small group meeting, and these are so important, I'm going to give a chapter to each. Here they are:

1. Worship
2. Bible study
3. Sharing

4. Prayer

5. Accountability

One of the functions of the leader is to decide ahead of time what portion of the time to give to each, and in what order they'll come. It ought to be different every time, so there's the fun of freshness to each meeting. And the working out of each of the five ingredients should be different each time. More on that later.

Suppose the first time you spend the first ten minutes in worship. The next time open with Bible study, or something else. Suppose you open one time with singing. (Why not? Jesus' "small group" sang together in Matthew 26:30.) Then the next time perhaps you'll open with prayer. If for the last six times you've bowed your heads to pray together, next time try it on your knees, or kneeling in a circle holding hands. The Holy Spirit will give you lots of ideas for variety.

And don't use the same number of minutes for each ingredient each time. Recently one of Ray's groups spent their whole hour together in prayer. How good not to be rushed!— really to linger before the Lord! They'll probably never forget that time together.

In one sense there must be structure to get anything done. But on the other hand, you never know when someone will come in a crisis, or having a special need, and plans must be dropped to give that person all the time he wants. We've discovered in our couples' group that it seems about once in every five or six meetings, somebody's need for prayer and concern is so great, the others have to shelve their requests until next time and give themselves to that person. And, my, how our needs are met, in that loving circle!

And then there was the time when a group of disciples gathered at our dining table, and one of them spilled the news that that week she'd had a phone call from an unknown voice who said, "This is your real mother." And Dotty, who'd been adopted as a little girl and had grown up contented and happy with her adoptive parents, suddenly had to greet in her living room another mother and a new stepfather; and now she must adjust the family life to a third set of grandparents, not to mention conquering the feelings of her own heart. How Dottie soaked up the support and prayers we gave her that day and through the weeks to follow!

Or another time a group of mine gathered—to discover that Ellen's father-in-law, who is senile, had been missing for twenty-four hours. So the loving act of the morning was to dismiss the meeting and drive around Pasadena hunting for a missing person so precious to our sister. P.S. He was found, unharmed.

You never know what the emergency may be, so the leader, with all his plans, must be sensitive to adjust—a little or a lot.

On the other hand, all of us dearly love to talk about ourselves, and the sharing can gobble up all the time unless it's tactfully controlled! This is another wonderful exercise in the disciplines of relating to each other in the "family." We learn give and take; we learn to submit to each other, at close range; we learn to consider each other better than ourselves, even in what we share and how long we take to share it.

A "cell" time together is not a meeting with a roll call and reading of the minutes of the previous meeting. It's the gathering of a living organism, a part of the Body of Christ. It's the sacrament of a family conclave, with all the communication needed to keep the relationships cleansed and edifying. So the leader plans, and then uses his plans or not as the Holy Spirit directs.

Now let's consider each ingredient of a small group gathering.

13.

Ingredient One: Worship

It's easy for groups to be totally horizontal unless they deliberately look up. Jesus said, "Where two or three are gathered in my name, I am in the midst." That's thrilling! The key is *in his name*. Then it's not just your average kaffeeklatsch.

Be sure that you have the great privilege together of just giving God pleasure! Tell him who he is. Tell him why nobody, nothing else, compares with him. Tell him this group is for him. For most of us Christians, worship is our weakest muscle. We don't even know how, and we're awkward about it.[1] We end up saying "thank you" over and over. And mostly it's "thank you for doing this for me," and "thank you for doing that for me," and we've focused back on "me" again, instead of God. Worship and thanksgiving are not the same.

It's good to get out the Scriptures and use them for a guide, to get the hang of it: "Who among the gods is like you, O Lord? Who is like you—majestic in holiness, awesome in glory, working wonders?" (Exod. 15:11). "Sovereign Lord, you made the heaven and the earth and the sea, and everything in them..." (Acts 4:24).

Sometimes in our groups we just worship in prayer, but

here's a variation on that: sometimes we turn to a praise passage in the Bible and pray in sentences around the group, each taking a verse from that passage. We don't read the verse; we just use it as a springboard for ideas for praise. So when it's my turn to pray, I just open one eye and peek at my particular verse, and praise the Lord based on whatever comes to my mind quickly off the page.

Here are some passages which are wonderful for groups to use in praising the Lord through prayer:

Exodus 15:1–18

Deuteronomy 32:1–12

1 Samuel 2:1–10

2 Samuel 7:18–22

2 Samuel 22:2–4, 50, 51

1 Chronicles 29:10–13

Nehemiah 9:5–8

Psalms 8; 9:1–11; 29; 33:1–12; 46; 47; 66:1–8; 84:1–4, 11, 12; 89:1–14; 92:1–8; 93; 95:1–6; 96; 97:1–6; 98; 99; 100; 103; 104:1, 2, 31–35; 105:1–7; 106:1–3, 47, 48; 111; 113; 115:1–3, 16–18; 135:1–6; 145:1–13; 146; 147:1–11.

Isaiah 15:1–9 (First explain verse 2 by chap. 24—final punishment for sin)

Isaiah 40:21–26

Luke 1:46–55

Romans 11:33–36

Revelation 5:12–14; 15:3, 4

Or bring hymnals together, and in unison read through one of the worship hymns in prayer.

Or adore God the way Song of Solomon teaches adoration ("You're an apple tree among the trees of the forest"; "You're a lily among thorns . . ."). Just take turns praying, "Lord,

You are—" and fill in the blank, maybe with adjectives, maybe with nouns. You'll never run out!

But worship doesn't have to be prayer. It's just exalting God and focusing on him. How many ways can you think of to do it? Sometimes our church collegians go through the alphabet naming an attribute of God that begins with each letter.

How about studying the form of Psalm 107 for your Bible study together? You'll discover it has a beautiful structure:

> Introduction: verses 1–3
> Stanza One: verses 4–9
> Stanza Two: verses 10–16
> Stanza Three: verses 17–22
> Stanza Four: verses 23–32
> Conclusion, verses 33–43.

Each of the stanzas tells about a different group of people and their particular need for the Lord. And each stanza ends, "Let them give thanks to the Lord for his unfailing love . . ." and so on.

Then for your worship time, make up a similar psalm in the group:

Read the introduction in unison.

Let each member make up a stanza orally, describing a group of twentieth-century people who need the Lord. He can end the stanza with the same refrain Psalm 107 uses.

Then everybody reads the conclusion in unison.

Or for another worship time, notice Psalm 136, which tells of things God has done in history to be gracious to his people, and then tacks on a half-sentence refrain. Go around the group creating your own psalm with this format, each saying one way God has acted for his people—maybe for your church —and all in unison repeating the Psalm 136 refrain.

Or look at Psalm 147:12–20. It begins and ends with "Praise the Lord," and in between describes God's mighty acts, either in nature or to people. So your group can begin and end with "Praise the Lord!" and in between, offer single sentences of what he's done. You'll discover you're chuckling with fun, and there'll be looks of glory on your faces!

Or Psalm 148 commands different created beings to praise God. Make up your own group psalm doing that!

Or sometime, for your act of worship, simply take five minutes of quiet while each person composes his own psalm of praise to God: maybe a four-line poem which may or may not rhyme. Then take turns reading them out loud.

Or sing a pre-chosen hymn of worship together, with or without piano. Maybe somebody could have done a little homework to find out about the author or composer first, and how the hymn happened to be written.

Or for your Bible study, dissect the words of the hymn, finding Scriptures that relate to it, and then sing it for your worship time.

Or how many other ways can you think of to exalt the Lord together?

14.

Ingredient Two: Bible Study

Charles Wesley was called a "Methodist" because he used "methods" to create an atmosphere in which the Holy Spirit could work. And what was his method? Small groups! He called them "class meetings," and under his direction thousands of class meetings sprang up all over the English-speaking world of his day.

His suggested "methods" were very precise:

1. The people were to meet once a week, to confess their faults and pray that they might be healed (James 5:16).

2. There were to be five to ten in a group.

3. They were to begin with singing and prayer.

4. At each meeting, each member was to speak of the temptations and deliverances he'd experienced since their last meeting.

And so on. And the result? Revival!—and the birth of a huge Protestant denomination.

Charles Wesley loved God's Word and preached it with great fervor. But he didn't make the emphasis of these class meetings Bible study. He knew that they needed plenty of that in other places, but the point of these gatherings was to be the sharing of lives, with accompanying confession and cleansing.

We have the same need today! Church preaching, Sunday school classes, Bible classes, books, tapes, radio and television preaching, and much more are available to feed us the Word of God, and we need to be immersed in it! It will be the basis of everything else we do, for by God's Word we grow in knowledge of him and his will for us.

But those things are all informational, and a small group should not be primarily that. If it were, it could have five thousand members and rent a convention center for its meetings, because all that's needed for information is one person standing up in front, teaching.

But for Christians to get eyeball to eyeball with each other, with all the loving realism between them which God intends, four to eight people (Wesley said ten) is enough. And you mustn't think of your gathering as first of all a "Bible study" or a "study group." With all the biblical and theological facts available to be poured into us, hiding our true lives behind more "study" may be a pure "cop-out"! You really don't need curriculum, and if you get to filling in too many blanks and assigning too much homework, your personal lives may get overshadowed. So watch it.

Nevertheless, we *do* need God's Word, and it will cleanse and purify and set the tone of your gathering every time you're together.

And probably you don't want to wait until you're together and then shut your eyes and let your finger stab a Bible page at random! So what will you study?

It may be simply that the leader picks a passage that's been meaningful to him the last week, has the group read it, and then turns them loose on a 20-minute discussion of what they see in it. Rich things will surface! If you've been gathering Bible study notes in a notebook and then transferring them to a file,[1] you don't need any further suggestions from me. You already have a growing accumulation of riches to share!

But several times in groups we've been helped by studying leadership as seen in the life of Moses from the Book of Exodus. I'm including my notes here on that study, in case you'd like to "borrow" them. Just take a passage or two each time and discuss them together, with no planned cut-off place so that you can quit whenever you run out of time.

Help yourself!

Introduction: Moses' pre-leadership days

Exod. 2:11–15: Started out "doing what came naturally;" no promise of leadership.

3:11: In first confrontation with God, no confidence in God's ability to work through him.

3:13: Faulty understanding of God.

4:1: Spirit of fearfulness, timidity.

4:10: After seeing two great demonstrations of God's power, unwilling to obey because his attention is still on himself.

4:11–13: When God verbalized his power to make it crystal-clear, Moses still unwilling.

4:16–18: Fantastic compassion of God: he had still chosen Moses for leadership, but was willing to accommodate himself to Moses' fear, let Moses' brother do the talking for him. (6:10, 11: Gave Moses still another chance. 6:12: Moses still reticent. From 6:13 on, Aaron is the mouthpiece, but in 32:1–6, 25 he is also a thorn in Moses' side. Also his sons, Lev. 10:1, 2.)

Forty-year accommodation. Only when Aaron finally dies (Num. 33:38), does Moses discern God could give him eloquence. Book of Deut.: Moses' speeches after Aaron's death! See Deut. 32:1–3, etc.

Leadership as Seen in the Life of Moses

REFERENCE	PRINCIPLE
Exod. 4:21	God will reveal all the circumstances we need to know for leading.
4:27–31	When we are quick and unquestioning in our obedience to God, the people will often respond.
5:1	"Thus saith the Lord": the authority of leadership.
5:1–12:32	Great struggle against sin, with unflinching persistence, will finally pay off.
5:22–23	During the course of the struggle leaders must not draw hasty conclusions and become discouraged.
Exod. 7:7; Deut. 34:5–7	Effective leadership can begin and end at any age. If God gives a position of leadership, he will also give all strength needed to carry it out.
Exod. 7:9–11	It's important to be steadfast in God and not be discouraged when we see Satan's followers imitate our leadership.
Exod. 7:12	God will have his own ways of reconfirming our position in spite of it all.
Exod. 8:18; 9:11	And if we continue steadfast, eventually we will see that "greater is he who is in us than he who is in the world."

REFERENCE	PRINCIPLE
Compare 8:9–10; 8:15–19; 9:17–30; 10:3	As we exercise leadership in direct confrontation with sin, God will increase our boldness and effectiveness.
Compare 10:9–11; 10: 24–26; 12: 31–32	When God has given orders, people must not be allowed to pressure us to compromise.
Chap. 11	A leader must prepare his people for what is to follow.
12:28, 50	Quick and unquestioning obedience by leaders sets the tone for followers to obey also—obeying both God and God's leaders.
13:17; 14:1–3	When we are sensitive to God's directions for leading our people, we will be delighted at the kindness and wisdom of his strategy.
13:21–22	Although God's use of human leaders is very real, his own personal leadership over all must always be visible.
14:10–11	Leaders must never be surprised when they have to take the impact personally of people's rebellion against God.
14:13	When leaders truly represent God, they can encourage his children to great acts of courage.
14:13–15	Simultaneously, as leaders lead with a great show of boldness, behind the scenes God will be dealing with their own secret fears.

Reference	Principle
14:15–31	When God is leading us, he takes care of every detail and sees us through to the very end.
14:21	One small act of obedience, calling for very little strength on the part of a leader, will be accompanied by God's great demonstrations of power.
14:24–25	World political and governmental circumstances are ultimately ordered by God. Leaders must *work* as if all depended on them, while at the same time mentally *resting* in the fact that all depends on God.
14:31c	Amazingly, God allows his leaders to be identified with himself, and to share his glory.
15:1–21	After people have experienced great victories, leaders must allow opportunity for great celebration—as a means of praising God, and to impress it all in their memories. . . .
15:24, 27; 16:2–3	Nevertheless, leaders may expect masses of people to have short memories, and to change moods quickly with each new situation.
16:19–20	Godly leaders can expect to be angry over what angers God, and to increasingly share his emotions.
16:25–28	The price of leadership: a leader is personally responsible for seeing that his followers obey.
17:4	As Christ our Leader took the brunt physically for all the sins of the world, so human leaders may have to take the brunt physically for the local sins around them.
17:8–13	A leader's job of intercession can get very heavy. It's important to bring in close brothers

REFERENCE	PRINCIPLE
	who will share the burden and thus also learn leadership.
18:9–19, 14	No matter how qualified the leader, he needs advice from a godly outsider who can see the situation more clearly.
18:17–23	Delegation of responsibilities is essential to keep the burden of leadership at a manageable level.
18:25	The reflection of a good leader is the ability of the men he raises up around him.
19:7–9	A good leader represents God to the people in his public life; but in his private life he must also represent the people to God.
19:10–15	A leader must be aware of group climax times, and prepare the people to be ready for them.
20:19	A good leader, although representing God, must identify with his people as a true human being, so that they will relate to him. . . .
24:1–2	Nevertheless, whether the people are close to God or not, he must be consistently close.
25:1–8	Good leadership involves urging the followers to commitment of themselves and of their material goods.
Chaps. 25–30	God's Detailed Instructions.
Chaps. 31–35	Interlude of Terrible Sin.
Chaps. 36–39	The People's Carrying out of Every Detail of God's Instructions of Chaps. 25–30. Moral: A leader must not be discouraged over his followers' temporary lapses. If he continues

128

REFERENCE	PRINCIPLE
	faithful (including dealing with sin), days of obedience and glory may yet be ahead.
31:1–11	A leader may assume that whatever God expects a people to do, God will be responsible to raise up individuals within who have the necessary gifts. (If he doesn't provide the gifts, he must not want that particular work done.)
31:12–17	Under God, a leader must pace his people, allowing breathing spells.
32:9–13	When a sin is out of sight, it may not seem so bad. . . .
32:19–21	But when it's in view, the full impact of it should be terrible.
32:25–29	When lesser leaders blunder and the people are in confusion, it's up to the top leaders to be utterly decisive and lead the way out.
32:31–32	The ultimate in leadership: caring more for the people's good than his own, whatever the cost.
33:4–6	Leaders may use visual things to create moods —for joy, for repentance, etc.—not to stimulate superficially but to reflect and emphasize what they're going through.
33:7	A leader needs to provide specific, measurable opportunities (places, times) where people can seek the Lord according to their personal needs.
33:7–10	A leader's "apartness" is important: not aloofness for its own sake but a sense of "holiness unto the Lord." Thus will he seem followable,

REFERENCE	PRINCIPLE
	and he must use this advantage to point them to God.
33:11	A leader seeks younger ones who have a special heart for God to become his disciples; he gives them special intimacy with himself to learn more.
33:12–18	A maturing leader can experience more and more boldness with God.
34:8	A leader's most important moments are behind the scenes with God.
34:9	A leader must continually be in intercession for his followers.
34:12	A leader must stay separate from other leaders who would weaken his position with God.
34:29	A truly spiritual leader is oblivious of his own spirituality.
34:30–31	A leader seeks to be warm and approachable to his people.
34:29–35; 2 Cor. 3:13	For the sake of God's reputation, a leader reflects all of him that he can to the people.
35:1–19	A leader must not only be God's spokesman, but . . .
35:29– 36:3	He must be prepared for heavy administration to see that those words are carefully carried out.
36:5–6	A leader relies on the reports of his "lieutenants" as a basis for further action.
39:40	The machinery of a people working together goes smoothly when all are obeying the com-

REFERENCE	PRINCIPLE
	mands of a God-directed leader. (16 times in 2 chaps.: "Just as the Lord had commanded Moses—")
40:16	Secret behind the scenes: Moses meticulously obeyed God's commands.
39:43	Commendation is important in leadership.
40:33	A leader must see a work through to completion.
40:34	The responsibility of leadership is great when we see that often all workers are identified together by the name of their leader.
40:35	When God's blessing is on the work of a leader, in actuality he must back off from his own work: it has become bigger than he is personally, by the glory of God upon it.

15.

Ingredient Three: Sharing

Ray, Nels, and I sit at the table for a meal.

"I see something white," says Ray.

"The salt," says Nels.

"No."

"The napkin," I contribute.

"Nope."

This goes on for maybe three minutes. Nels and I have named everything we can think of. "I give up," I say.

"Not me," says Nels. "The hooks on the window drapes."

"Nope," says Ray.

A few more tries.

"All *right*," says Nels. "I give *up*."

Ray is ecstatic. "The whites in your eyes!"

"Mom's are pink," howls Nels. "And mine are yellow! I've got jaundice!"

You can see our conversations can go very deep.

But also, these days for our family Bible study we've been discussing chapters of Barnhouse's *Teaching the Word of Truth*.[1] We take turns teaching each other, and this morning it was my turn, on a lesson about our bodies, souls, and spirits.

"How would you describe the body, Nels?"

"Well, it's ... uh ... it's like the bag that holds the marbles, okay?"

"I thought that was your head—"

"Watch it, Mom—"

"And how would you describe the soul, Ray?"

"Um, your personality ... that part of you that relates to other people, as opposed to your spirit, which relates to God."

Nels interjects, "Then animals would have souls."

"Exactly," says Ray, "but not spirits. They can love and hate and develop personalities, but they can't worship God."

"What part of us is instantly redeemed when we accept Christ?" I ask.

"That's easy," says Nels. "Our spirits."

"What about our souls?"

Silence. "It *tries*," Nels volunteers.

We look up 2 Corinthians 3:18. "It's being transformed, says Ray; "it's in process...."

And so the discussion goes on. The sharing isn't all that deep, but it's meaningful, as we learn of eternally important things.

On the other hand, once in a while we may really get down there. Nels came back earlier this week from a five-day camp for the church high schoolers. God had touched him in a real way, and as we drove along in the car he told us about a late-night experience of going out alone to cry bitterly over his sins. It's so special to have your big teenager willing to bare his soul, and I figured the best way to receive his story was to answer in kind.

"Boy, Nels," I said. "That was heavy, wasn't it! God does that to me sometimes, too. He got to me recently when I saw how arrogant I can be. I can act as if I have all the answers, and I don't realize at all how hard I am to live with. But God loves me so much, he'll bring along some experience, and pow! I see myself, and he brings me up short, and I bawl like a baby. He's not through with me yet, but he's helping me."

Now, in our family, that's meaningful sharing. And you can't schedule it or program it; you just have to be exposed to each other enough so that when God's time is right, you've got those precious moments to be real with each other.

And that's how it is in our spiritual family. James 5:16 says, "Therefore, confess your sins to one another, and pray for one another, so that you may be healed." Our Roman Catholic friends have a weekly session with the priest, so that confession is automatically built into their lives; but when do we Protestants ever confess? We sin regularly; we should confess regularly, and stay continually cleaned out and forgiven.

For most of us who live in cities, garbage gets collected once or twice a week. Do you remember what happened a few years ago when New York City had a garbage collectors' strike? How the stuff piled up! And as long as the temperature stayed below freezing it wasn't too bad, but when it thawed . . . ! That's the way many Christians are inside, because it's been so long since daily sins were confessed!

To whom do we confess? James 5:16 says "to one another" —Christians to Christians. But when and where? It usually isn't too appropriate to pop up in church between the announcements and the offering. This is a crucial reason for small groups! The whole family of God can get totally clogged with unconfessed sins unless each member has a select group of brothers and sisters around him to whom he can relate in meaningful ways.

Ross Foley, in his new book *You Can Win Over Weariness*, says that "professional listeners" can't help us too much because our confession to them is secret! He quotes a contemporary psychologist, O. Hobart Mowrer, who writes,

> If "secret confession" to priests and psychiatrists had a really good record of accomplishment, we should be glad to be spared the embarrassment of having the "ordinary" people in our lives know who we are. But the record is not good; and reluctantly, many people are today experimenting with open confession of one kind or another.
>
> When you stop to think about it, *secret confession* is a contradiction of terms. And it is not surprising that the attempt to cope with unresolved personal guilt by means of continual furtiveness does not work out very well. Should we actually expect much to come of letting a priest, minister, psychiatrist, psychologist, social worker, or some other "specialist" hear our sins if we continue to live the Big Lie with the people who really matter to us?
>
> . . . I am persuaded that healing and redemption depend much more upon what we say about ourselves *to others, significant others,* than upon what others (no matter how highly trained or untrained, ordained or unordained) say *to us.*
>
> It's the truth we ourselves speak, rather than the treatment we receive, that heals us.[2]

Mr. Foley goes on to say that "confession that breaks the shroud of our secrecy and leads us out into the open before God and a group of significant other people will liberate us from fear and guilt in a way that nothing else can." [3]

Several years ago one of the Lake Avenue Church pastors said to the others at a pastoral team meeting, "Hey, I've been meaning to ask, who's been getting the heavy load of counseling these days? Over the last couple of years not nearly as many people have come to me for counseling."

The fellows all looked at each other (there are twelve full-time pastors on staff), and every one of them said he was doing far less counseling than before.

Then it dawned on them that the pastors were counseling less since Lake Avenue Church had gone into small groups! With many hundreds of the people meeting in homes weekly with each other at meaningful levels, problems were getting talked out, advice given, sins confessed;—the saints were beginning to minister to each other, instead of depending on the pastors to do it all! And how much healthier the whole Body is! Problems are nipped in the bud, and dealt with in an atmosphere of closeness and love, rather than waiting until the problems are enormous and must be taken to a "professional" in a more artificial environment. Certainly there are situations still where only a pastor will do, but the "family" members certainly seem to be healthier than before we had small groups.

But there's this aspect of confession. When I'm speaking at conferences about small groups, someone will often ask, "Do I have to tell them *everything* about myself?"

That's an important question to cover. No, no, no! Small groups aren't for the purpose of airing all our dirty linen! They're to be *Christ*-centered, not problem-centered. Maybe it will be weeks or months before the first problem or sin ever surfaces. That's all right! Just worship and read God's Word and so on, and let everyone feel comfortable.

But eventually, when the brothers and sisters love and trust one another, real needs will emerge to be prayed for—personal needs—and some victory will begin to be experienced in lives where it had never been achieved before.

Like it is in the family: there you are, simply meeting regularly (in a physical family, most often around the table). You talk low-key most of the time. But even the commitment to *be* there gives it some glory: your very presence with each other says "we belong," even if the conversation's as silly as "I see something white," or as run-of-the-mill as "How would you describe the soul?"

But crises in lives come sooner or later, and you're still there with each other. You're ready to absorb some of the buffeting, mingle your tears and laughter, offer your advice, pray together, or maybe just hug.

16.

Ingredient Four: Prayer

Oh, how hard it is to pray! Isn't it?

It's hard to spend enough time in personal prayer.

It's hard to spend enough time in group prayer. Prayer meetings can easily turn into hymn sings, Bible classes—anything but prayer meetings! And if the leader even says, "Now we're going to pray," another twenty minutes will go to "sharing prayer requests," and there's practically no time left actually to pray.

Why do we have to fight so hard to pray? Because our enemy knows prayer is a powerful weapon against him. Satan's wiles are frustrated by six things: truth, righteousness, the preparation of the gospel of peace, faith, salvation, and the Word of God—and all of these, according to Ephesians 6:14–18, undergirded by and surrounded by and bathed in prayer.

I remember when missionaries in a foreign country said to Ray and me, "Not many missionaries attend our weekly prayer meetings. To tell the truth, they're really boring. If nobody's sick, we don't know what to pray about!" And without the powerful weapon of prayer, no wonder those missionaries were battle-weary and discouraged.

But the Lord was eager to help them; and he used us to show them how to worship as their first priority, and then how to care for one another's needs as their second priority, before they ever thought about doing their missionary work! And when the conference was over, those special and wonderful front-line troops for God were starting to get mended, and their times of prayer together were alive and meaningful.

I think one of the very reasons for a leader in small groups is so that prayer won't get cheated. And so that prayer can be given all possible variety, to be sure it's exciting!

How can your prayer together have variety?

First, put variety in your methods of prayer. The chapter on worship suggested quite a few ways for you to pray.[1] Certainly, when you've been sharing your current life-situations, that will be a natural time to pray for one another, sometimes right around the circle. And when special needs unexpectedly come up, get in the habit of saying, "Why don't we pray about that right now?"

My own feeling is that normally you'll have many short times of prayer during the course of a get-together, rather than just one longer one, and then occasionally, for variety, have a really big hunk of time spent in protracted prayer.

What if not everyone is used to praying out loud? Part of the time, let just the "pray-ers" pray. Other times have silent prayer. And other times the leader can ask one person to start and another across the circle to close. That way, they're not praying "around the circle" and putting somebody on the spot.

But pretty soon, he could probably suggest that the ones who haven't prayed out loud write their prayers in advance and read them. Usually it's just a matter of getting used to the sound of your own voice!

There should be other varieties of method. Sometimes pray "conversationally," back and forth, one sentence or so at a time.

Sometimes pray around the circle, each one praying for the one on his right, or on his left.

Sometimes pray in unison—either with memorized prayers like the Lord's Prayer, or read together from prayer books or hymnals.

Secondly, there should be varieties of subject. Don't always just pray for each other! Sometimes pray for your country, and specifically for its leaders, as 1 Timothy 2:1–4 tells us to do. Sometimes pray for your church, and specifically for its leaders, too.

And stretch out! Pray for missionaries and other Christian leaders you know. Hebrews 13:3 says to pray for prisoners and for those who are ill-treated. There are many unsaved to pray for, and nations who don't receive or know the gospel. . . . Break out of the "God-bless-us-four-and-no-more" mentality!

There should be varieties of posture. Why not? We need terribly to be freed of our inhibitions in praise and prayer. If you just begin praying in the ways the Bible suggests, you'll no doubt be entering new territory in your prayer life! You might make a study of this in your group:

2 Samuel 7:18   Exodus 4:31

2 Chronicles 6:12–14   Psalm 47:1

2 Chronicles 7:3   Psalm 134:2

Nehemiah 8:6   Acts 13:3

17.

Ingredient Five: Accountability

"I have a new friend," said Saskia recently, her face glowing. "Really, my old friend is a new friend."

"Help me figure that one out," I said.

"Well," said Saskia (she's Dutch; that's how she got a name like that), "you know how Donna's been gloomy for months. She's been so upset over Susie's marrying a non-Christian that it's all she's thought about. She's been really 'down' in our group; she'd lost all her bounce.

"Finally last week I told her. She's been different for so long, I just laid it all out. I told her we missed her! I said we were lonely for the old Donna, that it wasn't fair for her to stew over Susie until we all paid for it. I said there came a time when we were to let each other go, and not ruin our own lives in mourning. Susie has to answer to God, not to Donna. Donna had to see that."

"You loved her with tough love," I said approvingly. Saskia has a beautiful "meek and quiet spirit." I knew the confrontation hadn't been easy for her.

"Last night our group met," said Saskia, "and it was the old Donna. She was concerned about us; she was fun; she helped us. It was so neat!"

And there was a look on Saskia's face of real accomplishment. "You know, she needed what I told her. She hadn't realized what was happening. I was good for her."

"Of course you were," I said, with pride in Saskia, and joy in her joy.

And as for me, I wish I could stand on a hill and shout to all my Christian brothers and sisters, "Love me with tough love! I need you! I can't see things about myself that you can see! Please don't hold back on me! Do it gently—but love me enough to help me become more than I could ever be just by myself!"

That's part of what God's beautiful family is for, and we hardly know it. We've hardly begun to function yet. We haven't loved each other intimately enough to be secure enough to be "tenderly tough."

At this point, we Christians are more familiar with gossip than we are with "tough love."

We're more familiar with behind-the-back criticism, airing each others' faults.

We're more familiar with face-to-face blaming, the harsh and hostile pointing of the finger. We handle each other so roughly!

We know plenty about each others' failures, but we know almost nothing about "tough love." Galatians 6:1 is almost an unfamiliar phenomenon to us—the idea of humbly helping restore a brother from a fault of his, and so bearing each others' burdens.

Perhaps we don't know about all that because we're not "family" to each other. We don't know the security, the deep cushion of love that belonging to our spiritual family should give. It's only after we've acted out our familial love, and affirmed it over and over in a thousand, tender father-son, mother-daughter, brother-sister ways, that we're secure enough for "tough love."

I expect to see us get there within my lifetime! I'm excited about this book, and the possibility that God may use it to open the eyes of his children to their roles of being family members to each other.

Christian fellowship must not only be supportive but corrective. We're not close enough to heaven yet to assume we never need correcting!

To plant a garden but never weed it will produce a garden that's a mess. To fellowship in a group of believers without accountability and correctiveness will eventually produce a group of believers that are a mess.

Colossians 3:16 pictures a family scene as authentic as a bunch of Johnsons, or Smiths, or Wilsons, living a typical week in their midwestern suburban home. It says,

> Let the word of Christ dwell richly within you, with all wisdom teaching and admonishing one another with psalms and hymns and spiritual songs, singing with thankfulness in your hearts to God.

There's teaching in it; there's music; there's admonishing as natural and to be expected as a game of croquet—right along with thankfulness and all the "good stuff"! To inject more admonishing into a tense, hostile church today would be disastrous. But where believers have been truly "family" to each other, and acceptance and love are understood—in that environment, admonishing is an essential and natural part of the family life.

"Keep your hands off your face," I admonish Nels. In case he objects, I say, "Who's going to tell you if your mother doesn't? That's what mothers are for," and I give him a hug. Admonishing and hugs: they have to go together.

"Don't eat that dessert," one of my Christian sisters admonished me when we were out together to dinner with our husbands. I had asked my group to hold me accountable to lose three pounds. So if I'd objected, she could have said, "Who's going to tell you if your Christian sister doesn't? That's what sisters are for," and she could have given me a hug!

Do you see that there are two sides to this coin of "tough love"? There is *accountability to,* and there is *responsibility for.*

First I had voluntarily said to my sisters, "I want to be accountable to you. Help me to lose three pounds." Then one of them had to love me enough to voluntarily be responsible for me: "Don't eat that dessert." It takes loving action on both parts.

One of the brothers I know came to his group one morning wanting to be held accountable. "Guys," said Dave, "I've sold some property, and I have $4,000 to tithe. I want your wisdom on where to give it, and I want to be accountable to you to give all of it right away, so I won't be tempted to spend any." It was an act of submission to the brothers and sincerity toward God, and how precious was the time together, disposing of that money!

Accountability to and responsibility for each other must be voluntary, but they ought also to be expected. No Christian should ever say to another, "It's none of your business; you have no right—" Yes, we have the right! James 5:19, 20 commends the one who turns back the brother or sister from straying.

And this is a long-time principle. Psalm 141:5 says, "Let the righteous smite me in kindness and reprove me; it is oil upon the head; do not let my head refuse it. . . ."

Love me with tough love!

In Galatians 2:11–14 Paul gave Peter a real "going over"

for temporarily falling back into legalism. Did Peter despise him for it? Later in 2 Peter 3:15, Peter wrote of him as "our beloved brother Paul," and in 1 Corinthians 15:5 Paul gave Peter high status. They were both the better men for the heat and pain of that "tough love" encounter.

I think of Carl and Dewey loving a brother enough to go to him and say he was neglecting his family.

I think of Sharon telling a sister she must break her engagement to an unbeliever.

All of them qualified—according to Romans 15:14, where Paul writes, "I myself am convinced, my brothers, that you yourselves are full of goodness, complete in knowledge and competent to [admonish] one another." [1]

I think of another sister who was agitated over her friend's engagement to a non-Christian and told me she planned to write her a letter. This is a friend whom she sees several times a week. I passed on to her the advice Ray always gives me: Say only positive things on paper. If you have something tough to say, say it face to face, so it can be accompanied by a gentle voice, hugs, and by prayer.

And say *lots* of positive things on paper! Get into the habit of writing frequent notes of encouragement and love. In writing, your words will lift others, not once, but over and over. And when you're dead and gone, you'll leave behind only happy, positive evidences of your life!

So much for the general subject of accountability.

Specifically, how do we hold each other accountable in a small group?

Sharing will automatically cause some personal desires or needs to surface:

"I'm no good at finding the books of the Bible. . . ."

"I have this neighbor I see often who doesn't know the Lord. . . ."

"I feel guilty because I know I ought to visit my grandmother at least every other week or so. . . ."

These are cries for help. We're there to build up one another in Christ: that means improve each other. So as we catch the principle of accountability—and assuming that we are expressing lots of love and affirmation—we begin to volunteer help:

"Do you want me to hold you accountable to memorizing the books of the Bible? How many do you want to learn in a week's time? I'll hear you say them. . . ."

"Would it help if I prayed for you at certain times when you're going to see your neighbor, that God would help you share the Gospel with her?"

"How would you like me to remind you every other week about visiting your grandmother?"

Pretty soon when a group regathers, you'll begin to hear the words, "How did it go?" "Did you have a good visit with your grandmother?" "Hey, shall I hear you say Bible books today?"

There's been many a good thing I've done in my life which I never would have done in a million years on my own! But I knew that some sister or brother was lovingly holding a knife in my back . . . !

Sharing goals is a very measurable way to build accountability into a group. When a group is new, make one-week goals, then three-month goals. Eventually make year goals, and then life goals. For one thing, it will help you know each other so much better if you know where each other's heading, or at least dreams of heading. When you join your prayers with his or her prayers for those dearest achievements, you begin to feel close, and you begin to support each other in helping those things happen. And accountability comes when you begin saying to each other, "How's it going? Are you getting there? I'm praying. . . ."

These are the life goals of some young women in one particular group I've been in.

The first wrote,

1. Live with God—seeking him and his will, living in his presence, obeying the truth he gives me, and being controlled by the Holy Spirit.

2. Love people—encouraging them toward Jesus by my life and my involvement in their lives, actually caring for those the Lord puts around me, discipling those the Lord gives me.

3. Make Lou happy—satisfied with me and with our relationship and with himself. Encourage him to be maximal for Christ.

4. Be a lifelong example of a godly woman for Lou Anne and any other children we may have. Effectively disciple them to maturity in Christ. Give our children security, stability, and a passionate love of Jesus.

5. Be a teacher of God's Word, knowing it myself and effectively communicating it to others, and motivating them to love God and search the Word (Ezra 7:10).

6. By 1986 have studied every book of the Bible and have a good grasp of the whole of Scripture.

(That last paragraph is an excellent goal because it's the most measurable; in 1986 she'll really know if she got there or not.)

Here's another set of goals:

Spiritual. To know God and his Word well enough to not have to question if I am in his will.

To properly budget my time so I can memorize God's Word.

To live the life of a godly woman and be thought of that way when I die.

To seek after godly wisdom. The gift of the Spirit I try to develop.

To make a permanent spiritual impact on other women for eternity.

Family. To be a support to my husband. *Not critical* but loving and understanding of his problems before mine. Put him first and not manipulate him.

To seek for our daughters to marry godly men that love them and support them in a proper fashion.

To seek for our daughters to be grounded in
1. God's Word
2. A good evangelical church.

To teach them to minister in a church without being disillusioned when they find that people aren't perfect.

To have enough faith in God to let him direct their lives and for me to stay out of their affairs.

Career. To work at a job where my responsibility is to manage people.

To work in a position that pays well enough so that I will feel all my years of experience and work will not be in vain.

Personal. To practise what I have learned about grooming so that I buy proper clothes and will feel well "put together" at all times.

To be able to afford to have my home decorated properly.

To travel extensively.

Here's one more set of goals:

Priority One. To constantly become more familiar with God through his word by having consistent quiet times and prayer and by memorizing.

Priority Two. To be a supportive and loving wife to Wes, so that I will meet his emotional needs as well as his physical ones.

To be a godly mother to my children, so that they will clearly see that it is Jesus alive in me, and that He is the source of any good flowing out of my life.

To learn to give more freely to the monetary needs of the Body of Christ.

Priority Three. To become less timid about sharing my faith, particularly with people I don't know well.

To become more aware of and concerned for those around me who do not have a relationship with Christ.

To learn to play the piano well enough that we can enjoy it together as a family.

To write and have published in some magazine or paper three poems expressing my faith in God and bringing glory to Him.

There are other lists of life goals. Don't you see how I knew these young women more deeply, and they knew each other more deeply, after they'd written and shared their life goals? I would think they know themselves more deeply, too.

That group isn't meeting any more, but I hope an occasional question to each other is still, "Have you submitted any poems to a magazine yet?" or "What book of the Bible are you studying now, to get you ready for 1986? I still pray for you!" (It takes courage to write goals for others to see. But it's the way to really stretch and reach! And hopefully, others will feel responsible to help you get there!)

Another way to build accountability into a group is to pass out blank daily schedule sheets each week. The members' homework is to fill in everything they can think of that they'll be doing the week following their next get-together. That includes the mundane as well as the exciting and/or "spiritual"! They can put stars or arrows by a time that needs particular prayer, or they can even list on the left side their special goals or prayer needs for that week. When meeting time comes, each pair of brothers or sisters exchanges schedules, so two by two they're praying for each other continually through the next week.

Let me sketch out a hypothetical weekly schedule, so you can see how one might look.

We always begin the schedule on the day following our meeting day, so for a Thursday group, the calendar would start on Friday.

Live from moment to moment mort aware of the presence of God – so pray for that!

"GET IT ALL TOGETHER SHEET"

Three Priorities		FRIDAY	SATURDAY	SUNDAY	MONDAY	TUESDAY	WEDNESDAY	THURSDAY
I. Commitment to Christ A. Q.T. B. Worship C. Practice God's Presence Continually	M O R N I N G	6:30 Exercise 7:30 Breakfast Kids school 9 Quiet time 10 PTA Committee	8 Exercise 9 Breakfast 10 House Clean— Kids help in A.M.	6:45 Exercise 7:15 Breakfast 9:30 Sunday School 11:00 Church	6:30 Exercise 7:30 Breakfast, kids to school → 9:00 Q.T. 10:00 Laundry	→ ford shop	10:00 Bowling with friends from former neighbor— First – two not Christians Pray!	→ → → shopping errands
II. Commitment to the Body of Christ A. Small Group Supportive Fellowship B. Time with Individuals C. Sunday School P. M. Service	A F T E R N O O N	12 Lunch with Committee Shop for dinner	12:30 Lunch 1:30 Q.T. 2:30 finish house, fix Sunday dinner	12:30 Dinner 2:30 Q.T. nap 4:30 With Cal call on boy in jail. Pray!	Phone Christian sister to encourage her	Shampoo dog → I should clean out my closet; ask me if I did!		3:30 New neighbor for tea to invite to Sunday school. Pray!
III. Commitment to Work of Christ A. Witness B. Job C. Good Deeds	E V E N I N G	6 Dinner 7:30 High school football game	6 Supper Shampoo hair T.V.	7:30 Evening service	6 Dinner T.V. iron	6 Dinner Book off or help kids with home-work	6 family out to dinner 7:30 Prayer meeting	6 Dinner 7:30 our group! (Yea!)

AT THE CLOSE OF THE DAY, CHECK TO SEE HOW YOU KEPT THE TIME

If you had received this particular schedule, then all week long, as God's Spirit prompted you, you could be keeping a running conversation going: "Lord, bless Sue now as she's shopping; help her to use her money wisely. . . . Father, as Sue is home with the family tonight, give them a loving time together. . . . Lord, don't let her miss that closet this afternoon: should I phone her about it?" . . . Meanwhile, she'd be praying through *your* week.

The next meeting, trade schedules with someone else. You'll get to know everybody in the group a lot better when you know how they spend their time for a whole week. This is a great way for men to pray for each other through their job-related stressful times.

A refinement of this sometimes used by our groups is a kind of self-testing. Before you give your schedule away, color in blue every activity that fits the "Priority One" category; in red everything that is "Priority Two"; and in green everything that is "Priority Three." There will no doubt be a lot left uncolored, but you'll begin to get an idea of how eternally important your life is, what areas you're weak in, and where strong, and so on. Too many blank areas may show you're not filling your life with enough important things, or too few may show you're overloaded. And remember, how you spend your time reveals your *life;* it uncovers your desires, your goals, your weaknesses, your heart—the real you. And you'll have revealed the real you to your close friends, as they will have revealed themselves to you. You'll all have lots to pray about!

Tough love. I particularly need this chapter myself. One of my spiritual "babies" recently admonished me that I'm not very good at admonishing! I needed that. It's true; I'm "chicken." But she's so eager to grow, and when I withhold from her, she's the poorer for it. That's not fair to her!

"Tough Love" is also the name of a song I wrote, the chorus of which goes,

> Tough love in the Body, Lord;
> Oh, give me tough love for my brother!
> And may we love hard enough, sweet enough,
>   long enough
> For tough love for each other! *

Physical families have tough love. It's because they care so desperately about how each other turns out. They are so closely bound together that each's success is the others' status, and each's failure is the others' pain. So there's a lot of heat and dust and flak in there, in the process of "turning each other out"! Tough love is at work.

I believe God is going to help his spiritual family to be close enough to care enough—to identify enough to have enough tough love!

18.

Suggested Curricula for Discipling Men and Women

Ray keeps his notes for discipling young men in his brown notebook! For any fellows who want these as a springboard for ideas, he says I may pass them along. Here they are:

PURPOSE OF SMALL GROUPS

1. To be biblical. Men and women of Scripture lived together in Christ and operated their lives in team work (Acts 2:41–47).
2. To build one another toward godly living and satisfying Christian fulfillment.
3. To help others become reproducers and disciplers of those who become disciplers, so no Christian is on the end of the chain reaction.
4. To build the total Body and fulfill Matthew 28:16–20.
    a. Select carefully and from within a purposeful group: Sunday school class, board, neighborhood, etc.
    b. Meet regularly.
    c. Have a cut-off time—review it at 6 months, 12 months,

18 months—but ultimately break up to make new disciples.

Four phases of leadership seen in Mark:
1. I do it (Mark 1, 2).
2. I do it and they are with me (3:12).
3. They do it and I am with them (6:7–13, 30).
4. They do it and I am in the background (16:15–18).

CURRICULUM FOR SMALL GROUPS

1. Each small group about 4 to 8 people.
2. Each meeting, while using variety, should have in it worship, Bible study, sharing, prayer, accountability for witnessing.
3. Have a cut-off time and plan to start new groups.
4. Pick people for your group who you feel are
   a. Teachable.
   b. Available.
   c. Enthusiastic.

Study material for Three Priorities generally
1. Go through Mark 1–8 and see how Christ and the disciples worked out the 3 P's—"Three priorities." [1]
2. John 15.
3. John 17.
4. Philippians 1.
5. Acts 1, 2.

---

[1] See Raymond C. Ortlund: *"Lord, Make My Life a Miracle,"* 1974, Glendale, CA.

Passages on Priority One Alone
1. Psalm 139.
2. Psalm 63.
3. 1 Chronicles 23:30.
4. Romans 11:33–36.
5. Isaiah 40.
6. Revelation 5, 7.
7. 2 Chronicles 29:10–20.
8. Jeremiah 1:1–12.

Passages to Help You Grow in Priority Two
1. Ephesians 4:11–16—Our differing gifts—1 Corinthians 12.
2. Romans 12:3 ff.—Our mutual care for each other.
3. Philippians 2:1–3(LB)—Our love.
4. 1 Thessalonians 1, 2.
5. Titus 2:1–6; 1 Timothy 5:1–3.
6. Eph. 5:21—6:4—Family.
7. Acts 13—How to make group decisions.
8. Proverbs 19:20, 12:15—How to get direction from brothers; 8:32–36; Acts 20:28 ff.—Christ-wisdom.

Passages to Help You Grow in Priority Three
1. Matthew 28:16–20.
2. Colossians 1:28, 29; 4:3–6.
3. Acts 1:8 and other Acts passages.
4. 1 Timothy 2:1–8.
5. 2 Timothy 4:1–8.
6. Mark 2:1–12.

Study passages on how to disciple your wife
1. Ephesians 5:21–33.
2. 1 Peter 3:7.
(Disciple: influence and lead in a godly way.)

Study passages on how to disciple your children
1. Ephesians 6:1–5.
2. Proverbs.

PROJECTS YOU CAN DO TOGETHER

First, organize your notebook for your own life.
1. Read Brother Lawrence, *The Practice of the Presence of God.*
2. Write a psalm of praise and share it.
3. Lead your family in worship.
4. Write one prayer of praise every day for one week and share one.
5. Memorize:
   a. Ephesians 4:11–16.
   b. Colossians 1:28, 29.
   c. Acts 1:8 or Matthew 28:16–20.
6. Have partners and try to talk or phone and pray for one another daily.
7. Have some experience of outreach together so as not to get ingrown—evangelistic, social or Bible study.
8. Read through Acts and note all the times the believers worked in team.
9. Develop life goals.
10. Study the 3 priorities on your own, and write your own biblical life-style from the study.
11. Read *Lord, Make My Life a Miracle, Up With Worship,* and *Your Church Can Grow.* All three are on Lake Avenue Church.
12. With whom are you on a collision course and need to face?
13. Write a morning prayer.

His words are so sparing—and he disciples so well! And then there's my kind: I write out everything!

What do I do, when I disciple women? Well, I've never done it the same way twice; neither has Ray, because each group has different needs. So we start off with a "beginning format," and then seek to guide in more individualized ways as we get to know the disciples better.

The first time a new group of women gathers in our home, we settle in the living room and read John 1:35–41. That passage says that Jesus began discipling men by showing them his home. Apparently you learn a lot about people by seeing their "native habitat." Andrew learned so much that he told his brother Peter that Jesus was the Messiah!

I have to be careful here that you not think I think I'm some sort of Jesus. I'm not to draw people to myself, but to the Lord. I know that in me, that is, in my flesh, dwells no good thing. Nevertheless, God works through people, and as other women see Jesus in me, in spite of and even through all my faults and weaknesses, I pray they'll be encouraged to let others see Jesus in them! And that's discipling. Remember, discipling is not just an intellectual giving out of truth; lives must be exposed to each other. Jesus called his disciples to be *"with him."*

So the first thing I do in discipling is to say, "Here's the house. It's not perfect, but neither am I! Help yourself; look through the drawers and closets! If you see dust, that's part of the real me!" (Do you think I'm crazy? Anyway, Jesus loves me!)

Then what? We gather around the dining table, as we will from here on. Discipling includes some eating, right? Acts 2:42 says so. But keep it simple. . . .

Of course we all come with Bibles and notebooks. If you

have five in a group and each has three prayer requests, how are you going to stuff fifteen items in your head? And how can you remember everything you're learning about the Lord unless you write it down? How could you pass it on? Everyone needs a notebook.

We've already determined cut-off time. One time I tried a discipling group for an eight-week period, but we all decided that was just frustrating. Just as we really began to love each other and get all warmed up and loose, it was over. Usually my groups last most of a year.

And the discipler or leader has planned in advance what will happen the first few times together, allowing plenty of time for group interaction.

Here are the first five sessions of a group of young wives I discipled, which began by concentrating on Titus 2:3-5:

> Older women likewise are to . . . encourage the younger women to love their husbands, to love their children, to be sensible, pure, workers at home, kind, being subject to their own husbands, that the Word of God may not be dishonored. . . .

So we divided up the first sessions into studying the role of women in their attitudes, in relationships with their husbands and children, in time management, in home management, and in money management.

Session 1: Attitudes

20 minutes: Looking around house together (John 1:35–41).

10 minutes: Praise together from 1 Chronicles 29:10–20.

20 minutes: Refreshments and study: 1 Corinthians 7:29–35. What was the temporary, cultural teaching? What

is the long-time principle for attitudes?
1 Timothy 2:9–15; 3:11.
Homework: Be able to answer "yes" to the last four questions asked in 1 Timothy 5:10 (not cultural applications, but long-term principles).
20 minutes: Sharing our lives: what needs praying for or rejoicing over
15 minutes: Prayer around group for each other
5 minutes: Ask for volunteer to lead worship time next week. Chat a little.

Session 2: Relationships to husbands

25 minutes: Refreshments and chatting. Review of homework.
15 minutes: Disciple who volunteered led us in worship from Psalm 145:1–6, her own choice.
30 minutes: Study 1 Peter 3:1–6; Ephesians 5:21–33; 1 Corinthians 7:3–5.
Suggested projects and goals:
1. Strong prayer life for husband.
2. Planning for surprises, fun.
3. "Blessed hope" of the church: reunion. What can you do to welcome him home?
4. Read Song of Solomon, one other good sex book.
5. Put Ephesians 5:33, Amplified Version, on card where it can be seen daily.
10 minutes: Quiet while each writes down seven admirable qualities of husband. Then—homework: tell him one of these things each day for next week!
5 minutes: Each pray for one on her right as a wife.
5 minutes: Assign one disciple to review for 15 minutes next time chapter 7 of this book.

Session 3: Relationships to our children

20 minutes: Refreshments and chatting.

5 minutes: Conversational prayer for this meeting and for each other.

25 minutes: Share around the circle the successes and good ideas we've found or heard of for raising children.

10 minutes: pray for each others' children by name.

15 minutes: Review of chap. 7 of this book by disciple previously assigned.

5 minutes: Discussion: how you feel you function as a daughter, sister, mother in God's family; how you'd like to feel.

5 minutes: Worship by singing and praying through the hymn "Holy, Holy, Holy."

5 minutes: Homework next time: bring your own housekeeping tricks to share; what irritates you; what you feel there ought to be a way to do better; and make out a week's or month's schedule of your housekeeping duties.

Session 4: Being a "Worker at Home" (Titus 2:5)

5 minutes: Worship from John 14:6: Divide group into thirds. In silence one group write down aspects of Jesus' being "the Way;" another third, how he is "the Truth;" the other, how he is "the Life."

10 minutes: Share these in discussion, and add others.

5 minutes: Prayers of praise for all these attributes.

25 minutes: Refreshments and sharing of our lives: where we are and what needs praying over.

10 minutes: Prayer for each other.

30 minutes: Share housekeeping tricks and schedules. Would one disciple volunteer to type and copy these

ideas for the group and bring them next time?
5 minutes: Hold hands and pray for each other for the week
to come.

Session 5: Money Management
20 minutes: Refreshments and discussion of our lives' weak
areas, from these sessions so far.
20 minutes: Each disciple suggest at least one area of life
(any area) in which she'd like to be held accountable
in some measurable way. Volunteers to hold each
woman accountable, until each has a new goal, and each
has a project to help another. Be sure these are written
in their notebooks, and all in the leader's notebook for
checking up.
10 minutes: Worship: Christ, our Wisdom. Read 1 Corinthians 1:24, 30 in as many versions as possible. Proverbs is the Old Testament book of wisdom, and thus
reveals much of Christ. Read around the circle the following, substituting the name "Christ" for "Wisdom,"
and "his" and "him" for "her": Proverbs 1:2; 1:20–
23; 4:7, 8; 8:12–36. In light of James 1:5, worship
in prayer the Christ who is our Wisdom. Revelation 7:
12!
30 minutes: Study Proverbs, our guide in finances.
A. Assurance of enough money: 10:3; 15:25.
B. Comments on having money: 10:15; 11:28; 15:
16; 23:4, 5. Conclusion: 30:7–9.
C. What to do with money.
1. Its purpose is blessing: 10:16; 11:24, 26.
2. John Wesley: "Earn all you can; save all you can;
give all you can."
a. Earn all you can: 10:4; 12:11; 13:11; 14:23;
15:19; 16:26; 20:13; 21:17.

    b. Save all you can: 27:23–27; 21:5, 20.

    c. Give all you can: 3:9, 10; 21:25, 26; 22:9.

  D. Make your goal to be a lender, not a borrower: 22:
7. When you do owe, 3:27–28.

  E. Don't get messy with your finances: 6:1–5; 11:15.

10 minutes: Conversational prayer that we will be good stewards of the money God gives us.

Now, I must say that there are a hundred other ways to start a discipling group probably much better than this, and these notes may not appeal to you at all. Maybe they're too detailed, or on the wrong subjects, or maybe just not your style. But if you want something just to get you going the first time, with these notes you'd be off and running.

Notice that if you begin one time with worship, begin the next time with Bible study or something else. If the leader has done a lot of the talking one time, make sure the disciples do, the next. If you spent fewer minutes in prayer one time, next time put in lots of prayer. Make sure you're making enough accountability happen. If you haven't sung lately, sing! And so on. Be creative; give it variety; give the disciples lots of opportunity for participation.

Other ideas for the discipler of either men or women:

1. The first time, give them your goals for the group. Sometimes I've said, "By our final session, I'm praying that you will understand and be living by the three priorities; that you will have formulated your life goals and you'll be living out of a notebook; [1] and that during our time together you'll communicate with each other in all thirteen of the ways the New Testament mentions." [2] To help that last happen, we'll probably make out a chart for ourselves.[3]

2. The first time together, have them make out a page in their notebooks for each member of the group. It's so con-

Roger, Christian

Jeep, 6½ accepted
Christ 2 yrs. ago
Jimmy, 22 mos.
Jodi, 6 mos.

MARY JENSEN
959 Santa Maria Dr.
San Marino 92225
529-9441
Jan. 21

4/28 Pray for their ministry to their friends
Dick, Jane who have separated
5/5 Jeep led Brian, first grade friend, to
Christ! Pray for Jeep to grow.
5/12 Dick, Jane coming for dinner. Roger
will attempt to reconcile. Pray!
5/26 Dick, Jane getting closer. Mary having
lunch today with Jane.
6/2 Pray she learn over summer how to
implement Isa. 58:10-12 in her life.
6/9 Mother ill: pray for Mary's encouragement to her.

Sunday School Class
couples' group

Sue Jamesian
neighbor

venient when you're praying for your brothers or sisters to have each of their profiles on one page. The illustration on the opposite page shows how one of my typical pages looks.

Mary is a dear friend from a former group of disciples. Her address, phone number, and birthday go underneath her name. (Here I faked them! You don't mind!) By the way, if a bithday comes up while your group is meeting, that's the time for some extra loving and fun.

In the upper lefthand corner goes the spouse's name, and whether he or she is a Christian or not; and in the righthand corner, any children, and whether they've received the Lord; it's important to know how to pray in the issues that mean most. In the lower left corner: any other small groups he or she may be in. In the right, any non-Christians currently a concern for witnessing—again for prayer support and accountability.

Then all the main part of the page is blank to begin with. But as we meet and that person shares needs for prayer, we date it and put it on the page. While we're meeting together the page becomes a spiritual diary of that period in his or her life, and cues for daily prayer. And it's great later, as your eye goes down the page, to get a quick synopsis of that friend's spiritual progress during that period, and how prayers were answered!

3. Another idea for one of the early times of meeting is to draw a graph of their spiritual lives up to that point. They can begin at birth or when they became a Christian, whichever they want. After drawing, they share theirs around the circle to help the group members get to know each other more deeply right away.

A graph that a man might have drawn might look something like this:

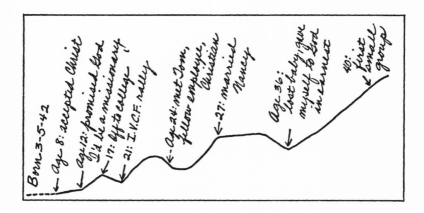

Suggestion 4. It's rare for these very special disciples of mine to miss a meeting, but sometimes children get sick, or there are out-of-town trips. When that happens, at the beginning of our session together one of those present volunteers to meet with the absentee once during the coming week to catch her up. She doesn't just give her the Bible study notes; for that she could use the mails. We are not just an "information group." She goes to her and actually *spends the time that we took together,* and seeks to make it a "happening." Together they worship; together they sing; they reenact everything that took place at the meeting, as much as possible. The volunteer fills the absentee in on the other disciples' sharing, and she teaches her the Bible study, so that when the absentee comes back, she really feels she is not behind. Part of our commitment is to experience everything *together.*

This system has at least two advantages. The group members think twice before they're absent. And they get experienced in discipling on an occasional basis before they're turned loose to do it regularly on their own.

5. On the last session of a group's meeting together, it's helpful, perhaps, to hand out a self-testing sheet, so everyone learns to do it better next time! This is the one I use:

SMALL GROUP SELF-TESTING

A. Ahead of meeting time I prepared myself by:
1. Praying I would come spiritually ready;
2. Choosing what to share: what contribution of mine would be of greatest benefit to the others (1 Cor. 14: 26).

B. I was present every time, except for very high-priority excuses which I made known ahead of meeting time.

C. I was on time every time.

D. In sharing I was not self-centered but others-centered—as proved by the fact that:
1. More often than not, the situations I shared were representative of common problems, so that solutions suggested to me might also help them;
2. More often than not, I lifted the group by being positive and encouraging (Eph. 5:18–20).
3. More often than not, my sharing was deliberately time-conscious.
4. More often than not, I weighed first whether to speak, equalizing my amount of sharing with others (Eph. 5:21).

E. During the weeks I prayed for each group member.

F. During the weeks I interacted with each group member at least once during our total span of time together.

G. I have deliberately "put feet" to my prayer requests by:
1. Witnessing to the unsaved for whom I have requested prayer.

    2. Coming to each meeting prepared to follow up with reports on previous requests.

H. I have taken others' prayer requests seriously by:

    1. Checking up on them where they asked to be held accountable.

    2. Including their requests in my prayer times.

I. Now that our group sessions are ending, I will:

    1. Evaluate what needs/prayer requests seem now resolved/answered, and how not to lose track of something in my life still pending. (Ask one member of the group to continue to pray for this?) (Next group I'm in take it up?)

    2. Categorize and file what I've learned, to pass on in the future.

    3. Ask God for those he would have me disciple next, and when; make specific plans and dates.

    4. Keep a special place in my heart for the members of this group!

These agenda and suggestions have been terribly detailed —which works well for me, because that's the way I am. But you notice Ray's is not nearly so detailed. The point is to be yourself, just the way God made you! Most important, share Jesus Christ and share your life in the way *he* leads you to do it.

And this chapter gives ideas for discipling, but perhaps you feel more inclined toward a "supportive fellowship,"⁴ a group of peers. Let each leader be as detailed or as "loose" as suits his personality and his gifts. As the Holy Spirit prompts it all, God will be glorified!

One final note about discipling groups and supportive fellowships. I have both kinds of groups in my life, and many people I know say they couldn't do without both. But if you must choose for time's sake between the two, choose discipling. By that I mean, if you're mature in the Lord, disciple others. If you're a new believer, ask someone else to disciple you.

The reason? Because discipling is the more specifically biblical of the two. In Matthew 28:18–20, Jesus' parting words told us to go disciple others, teaching them everything that he has taught us.

That's what immediately began to happen ten days later, in Acts 2:41 and following. And later it became Paul's lifestyle, and he told his disciples to do the same: "[Timothy], the things which you heard from me in the presence of many witnesses, these entrust to faithful men who will be able to teach others also" (2 Tim. 2:2).

This is basic, biblical Christianity. No Christian service can substitute for this: not directing the church choir, not ushering, not cooking church dinners—not even writing Christian books. Discipling is foundational; it keeps you in touch with God and with people, and keeps you bringing the two together. It keeps you growing in grace: your personality is challenged and stretched. It keeps you growing in knowledge: you automatically keep learning God's Word. It's God's plan for your life.

Have you been a Christian for a while, and learned a few things? Then you're responsible to act out your role as a spiritual father or mother in God's family. Gather those around you who have "heart," who are available, and who are teachable, and say, "Hey, how would you like to meet together once a week for a little Bible study, and to share our lives, say, through next June? Would that be possible?"

Or are you a "young" Christian who doesn't know much yet? You're responsible to act out your role as a child in the family. Go to someone whom you respect and say, "I really want to learn more about the Bible and about the Christian life. Would you take me on for a while and disciple me?"

So that you won't ever stagnate, there should always be a "flow" through your life. You should always be learning from those who know more than you do, and you should always be teaching those who know less. All of us are forever responsible to be son, brother, or father—daughter, sister, or mother—depending on the spiritual level of the one to whom we're relating at the moment.

Yes, all of us are forever responsible to "put it together" in the family of God!

19.

An Experimental Half-Hour "Walk-through" of a Small Group for People Who Want to Try It Just Once!

Bring your Bibles, and sit in a living room or around a table. Have only 4 or 5 in a group. Divide if there are more, and pick a group leader or leaders—that is, just anyone who'll read the directions off this page, and follow the clock!

1. *Worship: 60 seconds.*

In conversational prayer (anyone begin, and in any order) pray, "Lord, You are——" and fill in the blank with any word you think of. One sentence for each prayer. Each may pray any number of times, or not at all. Leader peek at the clock and end.

2. *Bible study: 10 minutes.*

Someone volunteer to read out loud 1 Thessalonians 5:11–18. Maybe someone else read again from another version. Then discuss whatever pops into your heads concerning this passage. Leader end.

3. *Sharing: 10 minutes.*

Each person share something in his personal life he'd like prayed for. Unless there's some overriding issue, let it be a need brought to mind while reading this passage. Everyone participate. Leader end.

4. *Prayer: 9 minutes.*

Maybe you'll want to hold hands, maybe not. Pray by name for each request. Everyone doesn't have to pray, but everyone must be prayed for!

* * * * *

Hey, that was good, wasn't it! Want to do it again sometime?

20.

Rearrange Your Life to Three Priorities

Here's a chart Ray and I have shown many times on overhead projectors at conferences. It helps us "get it all together." Maybe it will you.

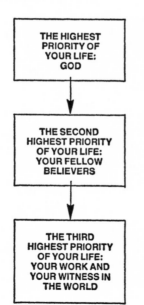

THE HIGHEST PRIORITY OF YOUR LIFE: GOD

PRACTICING HIS PRESENCE
DAILY QUIET TIMES
OCCASIONAL LARGER PERIODS OF TIME ALONE WITH HIM
REGULAR PUBLIC WORSHIP
LOVING GOD THROUGH FINANCIAL GIVING

THE SECOND HIGHEST PRIORITY OF YOUR LIFE: YOUR FELLOW BELIEVERS

DISCIPLING AND STRENGTHENING EACH OTHER THRU SMALL GROUPS (PRAISE, BIBLE STUDY, SHARING, PRAYER, ACCOUNTABILITY)
LOVING EACH OTHER THRU GIVING

THE THIRD HIGHEST PRIORITY OF YOUR LIFE: YOUR WORK AND YOUR WITNESS IN THE WORLD

EXCELLENCE OF LIFE AS A GOOD REPRESENTATIVE OF CHRIST IN THE WORLD
YOUR CHRISTIAN SERVICE
YOUR EVANGELISM
LOVING THE WORLD THRU GIVING

Kent is a huge ex-football player, and he's Minister to Adults on our church staff. He is one beautiful hunk of "God's man"!

"Ray," Kent said recently, "I've been asked to go to Rhodesia for ten days to teach African pastors." He spelled out the details.

"Goforit" said Ray. That's all one word around here. Ray was thrilled as all our church family was thrilled. Spreading the philosophy of the three priorities around the world is exciting for our church.[1] We not only go out to tell, but we have seminars for pastors and lay people here on our campus.

Last month Ray and I took a lay couple to Japan and Taiwan, where the four of us spoke to missionaries about the three priorities. Wonderful front-liners for God that they are, missionaries can get exhausted putting "priority three" first. Without taking the time for meaningful worship, their spiritual lives dry up, and without taking the time for deep interaction with their fellow believers—missionaries and nationals both—they get terribly lonely.

("But we have target dates to get the Scriptures translated, and there's simply no more time!" objected talented, outstanding missionaries in Peru. "Then postpone your target dates!" we said. And God put them together in genuine revival which is still going on years later.)

In January, the Lord willing, Ray and Nels and I will tour a number of the countries of Africa for seven weeks, ministering to missionaries in just this way.[2] It is exhausting; it is thrilling; it is rewarding to see God's servants as they reshape their lives to his highest commitments.

And do you know, even the best-intentioned small groups can just settle into "priority two." We can get so comfortable with each other, we forget to stretch at both ends.

Individuals must learn to be well-rounded in all three priorities. Small groups must learn to be well-rounded in all three priorities. Churches must learn to be well-rounded in all three priorities!

Worship never automatically happens. It doesn't happen at all unless we hunger for it and consciously program for it. In our individual life, and in our small groups, and in our church, we must first stretch upward to God! Tell him he's wonderful; focus on him alone; name his attributes; tell him there is no God like him; praise him and love him.

Worship takes time. In your personal life you have to schedule when you're going to be face to face with him alone. Your group must schedule worship, too, or you won't do it.

Do you know anyone like this fellow? At his wife's funeral, he said, "Mary was a good cook. She kept the house nice, and she raised our kids pretty good, too. She was a good woman. I almost told her so once."

Here is an amazing thing: I was so eager to write this morning that I came straight from the breakfast table and started in —without having my own time of praising the Lord. But it was no good. Soon I was so convicted, I was saying, "All right, Lord! First things first! I can't write it if I don't do it!"

So first I wrote a prayer of praise to him, and then I turned to his Word. I'm reading through the Bible again this year, and today's reading started me in the Book of Daniel. Here was a young man whose life was strong in worship of God. Chapter 6 describes his custom of actually getting down on his knees three times a day to give thanks to God. And in chapter 2, we find Daniel in danger of getting his head chopped off, and yet in this unsettling situation he spends time in worship. I notice he refers to God thirteen times in three verses; young Daniel's thoughts are full of the Lord!

"Praise be to the name of God for ever and ever,
   wisdom and power are his.
He changes times and seasons;
   he sets up kings and deposes them.
He gives wisdom to the wise
   and knowledge to the discerning.
He reveals deep and hidden things;
   He knows what lies in darkness,
   and light dwells with him.
I thank and praise you, O God of my fathers:
   You have given me wisdom and power,
you have made known to me what we asked of you,
   you have made known to us the dream of the king."
(Dan. 2:20–33).

Worship is not something we do as a luxury when we have the time in addition to other things we have to do. Worship is the very stuff of life, and while we are worshiping, God is working on our behalf and taking care of many things for us that we need to do—more than we could dream. And when we are busy and we worship, God is gently forcing us to live by faith, and to believe that he is making up the time!

Then I read Daniel 4. The whole chapter is a remarkable testimony given by one of the most powerful emperors in world history, to tell how the only true God wouldn't let him go until he learned to worship! It is humble; it is honest.

Nebuchadnezzar, King of Babylon, writes a memo to "the peoples, nations, and men of every language, who live in all the world"—his subjects—and tells the story of the recent years of his life. He frankly admits how Daniel had warned him to drop his pride and become an obedient believer in the one true God. He shares how instead he got even prouder—until God gave him a nervous breakdown that lasted seven years. Then he tells how God finally gave him back his sanity so that his pride could give way to praise. And this great secular ruler writes to the known world,

> "I praised the Most High; I honored and glorified him who lives forever.
> His dominion is an eternal dominion;
>   his kingdom endures from generation to generation.
> All the peoples of the earth
>   are regarded as nothing.
> He does as he pleases
>   with the powers of heaven and the peoples of the earth.
> No one can hold back his hand
>   or say to him, 'What have you done?' "

By one way or another, the wonderful "Hound of Heaven" is seeking to bring us all to the point of *worshiping him.* He is not satisfied with anything less than that—and deep inside us, neither are we. We will be selfish, irritable, and frustrated until we learn to make a habit of looking up into his face and telling him with our words that he's wonderful!

Thank you, holy Father, that in the midst of this writing you made me stop and worship you again! And I pray that these words from your holy Scriptures will feed and draw each reader back again to your feet in worship. You are the point of it all; you, and you alone, are "priority one"!

Friend, think about your own personal life. "Priority one" must come before "two" or "three." Unless you are rich in him, your sharing with your brothers and sisters will be thin and puny and horizontal. Have you ever been put on the spot and asked to share some "goodie" you've found in the Bible, and you say, "Ah . . . um . . . uh"? I have! Or found yourself in a group taking valuable time, but have it come out as inconsequential babbling—? I have. But God draws us together in Christ's name for better things than that.

Believers who are rich in God and in his Word behind the scenes will have lively, important conversations with each other when they get together. Out of "priority one" will flow "priority two."

And out of "priority two" will flow "priority three." I have never had much success in bringing other people to know the Lord until I had loving brothers and sisters on my back! I'd try to say something and the words would come out all wrong, and I'd feel like a total fool!

But these last few years my brothers and sisters have had specific names I've given them to pray over, and they hold me accountable. Boy, do I need that! And at last God is giving me some success!

So not only does "priority one" need to be deliberately built into a small group, but so does "priority three." Together you must reach up to God, and together you must get a heart to reach out to others. Out of "priority two," help each other stretch to "one" and "three"! The question is, how?

Well, of course you must pray for each others' witnessing. That lower right hand corner of my sister's pages in my notebook is my call to pray for her success in evangelism, as well as in the rest of her life. All of us need that! If I'm to pray for my sister to become a well-rounded, whole person, I must pray for her success in putting Christ first, her success in putting Christ's family second, and her success in serving him well and in reaching others for him.

And then, accountability! When she's given me names to pray for, I must be responsible to ask, "How's it going? Have you had contacts with these certain people lately? I'm praying—"

But beyond these things, let me suggest two ways that evangelism can be built into small groups.

"Supportive fellowships," at least—groups of peers meeting together—may decide to expect to draw new ones into their group from time to time. Perhaps every other month or so a new one or new couple can be invited in and absorbed. How blessed would be the church full of small groups expecting to take in the new Christian "babies" being born in that church! The new believers would get so loved and taught, they'd almost never fall away.

And the groups would get new freshness. It's so exciting to have a new "baby" in your midst! And when the groups grew too large, they'd simply split, with half the strong ones going to one and half to the other—by mutual consensus.

Here's another suggestion for building in "priority three." Our five couples meet every Thursday night except one. On the third Thursday evening of each month we are the praying "core" of a much larger evangelistic meeting called "Search." Maybe ten to fifteen couples gather in somebody's living room, and Ray leads a very "hang-loose" discussion Bible study. It's strictly geared for all those beautiful people who don't know the Bible and who probably don't attend church, but maybe are curious and feeling a need in their lives and would come to something like this if invited. The food spread is lavish, and there's plenty of laughter; we're trying to lure the fish with the best possible bait!

And it's exciting to count all the men and women who've accepted Christ right in the middle of our discussions or prayer —while the believers are silently, fervently praying, and the others are taking it all in!

"Search" is our "together project," so the five of us couples have plenty of names to pray over when we meet together. And the names aren't just "prospects"; they've come to be our dear friends together.

I had a note in the mail this week. It was from Elaine, who received the Lord in our living room a while back in "Search." She had just read *Disciplines of the Beautiful Woman,* and she wrote, "Several years ago you and Ray and the others brought joy and meaning into my life. . . . Now you've done it again. . . ."

God is good! Praise his wonderful name!

Epilogue

How I'd like to be a Solomon! Ecclesiastes 12:9 says that "not only was the Teacher wise, but also he imparted knowledge to the people. He pondered and searched out and set in order many proverbs."

He searched out proverbs that were couched in the culture of his day, and that's why with each proverb Solomon's people read, I think they said, "Ow! He hit me again! . . . Zing! I felt that one. . . . Pow! I gotta do something about that. . ." They must have gotten jolted and inspired and motivated all over the place. What a book!

Verse 10 says, "The Teacher searched to find just the right words, and what he wrote was upright and true." May the words of this book be that: biblical, balanced, in proper proportion. All of us, readers and writer, want to learn truth.

Saskia asked me recently, "How's the writing going?"

"Uh, well," I said, "I don't know how to answer that. I think the Lord's given me things to say, but maybe it's too heavy, the way I've written it. Maybe it doesn't have enough sparkle."

"I'll pray for sparkle," said Saskia.

Saskia, keep praying for sparkle! Solomon couched his truths in "just the right words." That's what I need.

But what am I doing, comparing myself to Solomon! I sit here in my old duds and bare feet, drinking water and eating grapes and pecans for energy, and I don't look, feel, or write like Solomon.

Then I read verse 11: "The words of the wise are like goads, their collected sayings like firmly embedded nails. . . ." And I think how when the Pentecost celebrants heard Peter's words "they were cut to the heart, and said to Peter and the rest of the apostles, 'Brothers, what shall we do?'"

And there came changed behavior! Lord, may this book move us to know your truth and to *do* your truth—tangibly, visibly, measurably!

I read Ecclesiastes 12:12, 13 with both a chuckle and a twinge of fear:

> Be warned, my son. . . . Of making many books there is no end, and much study wearies the body.
> Now all has been heard; here is the conclusion of the matter: Fear God and keep his commandments, for this is the whole duty of man.

I must not be writing-centered; you must not be reading-centered. We must both be God-centered! Back to God himself! Back to "priority one"!

"The conclusion is . . . : fear God."
He is the Source,
the Center,
the Fullness,
the Target,
the Completion,
of everything, everywhere . . .

of the universe . . .

of your heart in this moment.

As you're reading, tell him, "Alleluia."

There was a schoolteacher whose wife died, and he was left to be both father and mother to their one child, a twelve-year-old girl. Of course he was always bothered by the problem of not having enough time to give her, with teaching school; and he could hardly wait for Christmas vacation to come when they could be together every day for two weeks.

But the first day of vaction she was holed up in her room with the door closed, and only came out for meals. The next day was the same, and every day until Christmas. And the father could hardly get through the long, lonely days.

Finally came Christmas morning, and under the tree was his Christmas present: a pair of hand-knit socks.

"Daddy," she said, with her eyes shining, "I was so afraid I couldn't get them done in time! That's what I've been doing in my room—knitting you socks! Do you like them?"

"Darling," he replied, gathering her up in a big hug so she couldn't see the tears, "of course I do. They're beautiful. Thank you very much."

But in his heart he was saying, "Oh, little girl, I could buy socks anywhere. I really didn't want the socks, I just wanted you! I wanted your time and your attention and your love. I wanted to talk to you about things, and do things together with you!"

When we all get to heaven, do you think God will say, "Thank you very much for writing this book for me"; or "Thank you for reading it"; and "Thank you for all the ways you served me"—but that with tears he will add, "But I really didn't want you to do it at the expense of not having time just with me, myself! Most of all, I just wanted you! I wanted to talk to you about things, and do things together with you"?

We've come to the end of this book. Will you just put it down and walk away—and be the same kind of person you were?

I hope you'll give yourself in measurable, fresh ways to God. What will those ways be? He longs for your time, your words, your worship, your affection. Make him happy! I want to, too. Wherever you are spiritually, give yourself afresh to God.

Then after that—in the light of that—give yourself to his beautiful family, also waiting to be loved. They're all around you. They're lonely. They're hungry to know the Bible and grow; to be given time, to be patted and hugged and laughed with and cried with and counseled. They, too, want you, yourself! Nothing less will do.

And, oh, my friend, isn't it amazing that some day Jesus will even say, "Truly I say to you, to the extent that you did it to one of these brothers of mine, even the least of them, you did it to me . . . ?

"You loved the members of my family—you loved me. For them you inconvenienced yourself; you went without, to complete their material needs; you entered into my sufferings in order to fill them full; for them you endured hassle and strain—and your greatest joy was their maturity and completion. You shared my goals for them!

"Thank you! Well done! Enter into your rewards (did you dream they would be this wonderful?)! You make me so happy. Don't you understand now why, on my part, the cross was worth it all? Even the least saint is so precious!

"Let me give you another hug. You loved my family—you loved me. It wasn't easy; I know. I watched you every moment, and I interceded for you, that you would persevere. . . . And you did! I'm filled with exceeding joy. You identified with my sufferings; you were willing! Oh, my dear one!

"Come. We've both suffered; now let's go celebrate together." . . .

(Oh, oh. There goes my pencil point again.)

Anne would love to have you respond. Don't e-mail, fax or phone, but write to:

Anne Ortlund
Renewal Ministries
4500 Campus Drive, Suite 662
Newport Beach, California 92660

Notes

Prologue

1. *Disciplines of the Beautiful Woman* (Waco, Tex.: Word Books, 1977).

Chapter 1

1. Raymond C. Ortlund, *Lord, Make My Life a Miracle* (Glendale, Calif.: Regal Press, 1974).

Chapter 2

1. Quoted by Arthur Wallis in *In the Day of Thy Power* (Christian Literature Crusade, 1956), p. 34.

Chapter 5

1. The NIV says "house and line of David."
2. The NIV reads "all peoples on earth."
3. NIV marginal note: "or all fatherhood."
4. Russell Bradley Jones, *Gold from Golgotha* (Chicago: Moody Bible Institute, 1945), p. 37.
5. See p. 171.

Chapter 7

1. *Disciplines of the Beautiful Woman,* pp. 30–31.

Chapter 9

1. C. Peter Wagner, *Your Church Can Grow* (Glendale, Calif.: Regal Books, 1976), chap. 7.

2. Anne Ortlund, *Up with Worship* (Glendale, Calif.: Regal Books, 1975).

Chapter 13

1. Anne Ortlund, *Up with Worship.*

Chapter 14

1. See *Disciplines of the Beautiful Woman,* pp. 106, 119.

Chapter 15

1. Donald Grey Barnhouse, *Teaching the Word of Truth* (Philadelphia: Revelation Book Service, 1940).
2. W. Ross Foley, *You Can Win over Weariness* (Glendale, Calif.: Regal Books, 1977), pp. 126–27.
3. Ibid., p. 128.

Chapter 16

1. See pp. 117–19.

Chapter 17

1. KJV and NASB: "admonish"; NIV: "instruct."

Chapter 18

1. See *Disciplines of the Beautiful Woman,* chap. 12.
2. See p. 11 of this book.
3. See *Disciplines of the Beautiful Woman,* p. 117.
4. See p. 107 for the difference between the two.

Chapter 20

1. See Ray's books *Lord, Make My Life a Miracle* and *Lord, Make My Life Count* (Glendale, Calif.: Regal Books).
2. Time referred to was at time of writing; as of date of publication, the tour is an accomplished fact.

1524798R0

Printed in Great Britain by
Amazon.co.uk, Ltd.,
Marston Gate.